THE
GARDENER'S
BOOK OF

BERRIES

❧

THE
GARDENER'S
BOOK OF
BERRIES

❧

ALLAN A. SWENSON

L&B

LYONS & BURFORD, PUBLISHERS

PRINTED IN THE UNITED STATES OF AMERICA
DESIGN BY KATHY KIKKERT
10 9 8 7 6 5 4 3 2 1

SWENSON, ALLAN A.
   THE GARDENER'S BOOK OF BERRIES /
   ALLAN A. SWENSON
      P.   CM.
   INCLUDES INDEX.
   ISBN 1-55821-282-5
      1. BERRIES. 2. BERRIES—UNITED STATES. I. TITLE
II. TITLE: BERRIES.
   SB381.S94 1994
   634'.7—DC20   94-3179
                                               CIP

CONTENTS

TO RAYMOND BERGERON,
WITH APPRECIATION FOR HIS
GARDENING KNOWLEDGE, GOOD
HUMOR, COMMON SENSE, AND
FRIENDSHIP. EVERY GARDENER
EVERYWHERE WOULD BENEFIT
FROM KNOWNG A MAN LIKE RAY.

ACKNOWLEDGMENTS

During the many years that my family and I raised fruit and berries around our homes, we were actually designing our own fruitful landscape. It seemed easy and natural to plant some berry bushes here and there.

When it came to putting all those years into one book, I realized how many people had helped me over the hurdles—from my professors at Rutgers University, who suffered through my naive questions, to nurserymen, who freely offered valuable growing tips. Dozens, perhaps hundreds, of people have had a part in the preparation of this book.

To all of them, especially the dedicated men and women at the fruit breading and testing stations, and those with the Geneva Experiment Station in particular, I am indebted. Your efforts have helped make gardens and farms across America more bountiful. All of us who enjoy the fruits of our harvests each year appreciate your efforts. May your work in the future prove as abundantly fruitful for generations to come.

Perhaps the greatest joy of good gardening is the delicious bounty harvested from your own fruitful landscape. Talking with friends and neighbors over the past few years, I've noticed a growing desire to make gardens and home grounds more productive. There's an urge these days to become more self-sufficient, more capable of growing a wider range of plants, even in small backyard plots.

During hundreds of conversations, people have told me that they would like to plant more berry bushes, but they just don't have the room. It occurred to me, however, that there *is* a way to enjoy the fruits of gardening labors even on small plots. That's the premise of this book: You *can* have an abundantly fruitful home landscape.

During the past twenty years, I've interviewed many good growing friends around this country. I've talked with plant breeders and pomologists (fruit-growing specialists) who know their fruit business, farmers and orchardists, and legions of practical home gardeners. On one point we all agree: Berry growing isn't as difficult as most people believe. In fact, berry bushes thrive across America. For years, many of us thought that fruit growing required lots of space and special talents. That's not really so. With a little extra effort at planting time and some knowledge of how to prune, tend, and care for berry bushes, any family can enjoy a more fruitful living from their land.

The fact is, berry bushes are versatile. They fit well into outdoor landscapes. They provide appealing shapes and forms to grace our homes, gardens, lawns, and property lines. They can grow by themselves or in groups. Berry bushes have a variety of shapes and growth patterns that fit well into landscape plantings. So it seems logical to take advantage of the bonus that grapevines and berry bushes can offer us: tasty eating.

With those thoughts in mind, and with the help of hundreds of gardening friends and fruit-growing experts, I wrote this book. It isn't merely a gardening how-to book. It is designed to stimulate your appetite for more fruitful living as well as help you expand your growing horizons to enjoy the fruits of your gardening activities even more. Having lived in various regions and traveled to different parts of America, I've gathered the best information from many sources to include in this book. Each chapter is also based on my personal growing experiences, from way back to my youngest days on the farm tending acres of fruit trees to smaller home plantings in more recent years.

This book is dedicated to all of you who want to enjoy more rewarding, more productive lives. Multipurpose landscaping, using berry plants as part of your total landscaping plan, will provide that extra dimension. The bushes you grow are lovely to look at—food for the soul. The fruits of your harvest provide tasty rewards for the body: fresh fruit, pies, jams, jellies, and preserves.

On our home grounds, we're replanting and rearranging our gardens toward more fruitful productivity. It's both fun and worthwhile. I hope that you enjoy this guide to tastier living. Each tree you plant, each bush and shrub that bears some fruit, will bring you that much closer to a more flavorful, abundant life.

—Allan A. Swenson

With multipurpose landscaping, you can enjoy the blooms of berry bushes each spring, their fruits in season, and foliage in the fall. What's more, you can taste the difference a fruitful landscape makes as you and your family pick and eat fresh raspberries, blackberries, blueberries, and strawberries. Pies and cakes, preserves, jams and jellies, canned and frozen fruits and berries, plus wine and brandy are all extra benefits. So as you plan new landscape plantings or renovations of your present outdoor living areas, think fruitfully.

PLANNING YOUR FRUITFUL LANDSCAPE

Especially on small plots where space is limited, berry bushes offer greater versatility than decorative hedges. A berry bush or two can often be substituted for another type of shrub. Privet hedges are attractive and have their place in formal plantings, but a hedge of blueberries can be nearly as dense plus yield its bounty every year. In fall, unlike the privet and other types of hedges that merely drop their leaves, blueberries provide a red foliage display.

Spirea, bridal wreath, and similar flowering shrubs unfurl their distinctive blossoms every spring for glorious displays. Enjoy them if you like; they add a bright spot to your home grounds. But don't overlook some of the tasty berries that can grace a corner, frame a doorway, or line a pathway. Currants bloom well, though not quite as spectacularly as other flowering shrubs. When their tasty advantages are considered, however, perhaps a few currants deserve a place amid showier shrubs.

Property borders often pose a problem. Wandering cats and dogs may come to dig and mess your land. Neighbors may not share your appreciation for lovely outdoor living rooms that are well planted and tended. Blackberry hedges along your property line have several values. They conceal unsightly scenes, they thwart wandering animals, and they provide you with luscious berries that are seldom available in stores. Raspberry bushes too can form fairly dense rows to provide both privacy and good eating every year.

Good fences make good neighbors, to paraphrase Robert Frost. What better fence for making friends with your neighbors than a living, fruitful one that both families can tend and enjoy together? Sharing the cost of the plants, the fun of planting and caring for them, and the picking pleasure can bring neighbors closer together.

Grapevines are another tasty option. They climb and cling to fences, and their large leaves effectively hide areas that you prefer not to see. And as they do, their vines produce clusters of red, green, or purple grapes that are plump, juicy, and succulent. With grapes, you have more options. They can be trained to climb up trellises and arbors. With little effort you can build a shaded outdoor sitting arbor. Grapes, with a bit of training, will climb the posts and eventually flow across the top to provide you with welcome shade each summer. The best part comes as your vines begin to bear. Dessert for summer picnics is just a short reach away, hanging plump and ripe overhead.

If you have a long stretch of wall, try a fruitful hedge along it. The more natural growth pattern of living hedges breaks up the stark lines of long walls. Long hedges alone can also be striking and eye-catching parts of your plantings. Sometimes straight lines look good in more formal designs. Alternatively, weaving or bending the planting pattern can add an extra touch of grace to the overall picture. Blueberries lend themselves to a more tidily trained hedge effect than raspberries or blackberries. Blueberry bushes can be trained into graceful hedgerow plantings to block out undesired views of a neighbor's land, hide a compost pile or two, or separate one part of your yard from another.

Currant bushes in a row can be trained to a quasi hedge effect but they're more natural in rows of rounder, bushier plants. Even set alone, they perform their fruitful function here and there among other plants in beds and borders, along a fence, or in a group where they add their own distinctive shapes to a landscape.

There is a real value in blending different forms, shapes, and leaf patterns as part of a total outdoor scene. When you select furniture for a room, you look for pieces that complement each other but aren't necessarily exactly alike. Some standout accent pieces always lend a special touch. The same is true with outdoor living rooms.

There's no rule that says that fruit bushes must be planted in one spot, flowers in another, vegetables elsewhere. Masses of flowers planted in their own beds or borders admittedly have a striking and beautiful effect. Vegetables may be more conveniently restricted to their own patch, it's true. However, European gardeners who have small plots find that mix-and-match is a lovely and more productive way to achieve the most abundance from their land. New interest in this logical idea among American gardeners has increased recently, and for good reason.

When you have lots of room to spare, you can plant where and when you wish. But when space is precious, every square foot has to be as productive as possible. Berry bushes along a property line are fine, and you can add flowers in front of them for extra color in summer. If you have a stockade or other type of board fence, make it come alive with currants, blueberries, and gooseberries mixed with flowering shrubs in front of them.

Perhaps you have an unsightly corner that has been a planting puzzle. Consider that area for raspberries or blackberries. They can be allowed to wander in natural thickets, or sufficient pruning will keep them in bounds. Either way, you'll have put that otherwise wasted area to productive use.

Perhaps your driveway needs some added appeal. Most are barren stretches of pavement. How about strawberry beds along the hedges? Once you begin to think in multipurpose terms, you'll be surprised how far your imagination will lead you.

Evergreens are popular around many homes. Blueberries love the acid soil that is enjoyed by evergreens, including azaleas and rhododendrons. Why not plant some blueberries between your evergreens? They'll thrive in the same acid soil conditions and give you a bonus with their true-blue fruit.

The German writer Goethe once observed, "If every man swept in front of his own house, the whole world would be clean." A famous American nurseryman added to that thought not long ago. He's Paul Stark, Jr., of Stark Brothers in Louisiana, Missouri, our nation's largest and oldest nursery. "Few of us realize how important an abundance of trees is to man and his environment," Mr. Stark noted. "Right now, we are burning more and more fuel and upsetting more and more the healthful balance of oxygen and carbon dioxide in our atmosphere. For that reason alone, we should have more and more trees because they are nature's principal factories for converting carbon dioxide into oxygen." That idea also applies to berry bushes.

Berry bushes have another practical value. Real estate agents will attest to the fact that lovely shrubs add to the resale value of a home. Time after time it has been proved that a well-planted home with the same square footage, number of bedrooms, and facilities outsells one with only a few trees and shrubs.

Strawberries in window boxes, tubs, and planters are also interesting, and a strawberry barrel can brighten your home and delight your palate. Indeed, so can tubs or barrels containing blueberry or raspberry bushes.

Berry bushes should be one of your first investments as you begin to landscape your home. Once they're well planted, they'll grow and set permanent, deep rootholds to reward you for many years. As they grow, you can go about your other gardening activities, from arranging beds and borders to planting bulbs, flowers, and vegetables.

As you plan, remember these other benefits of plants: They buffer the wind, especially in winter. That saves considerable heating expense. They are also nature's best noise barriers. According to the U.S. Department of Agriculture and city noise-pollution experts, proper planting can reduce noise pollution by as much as 65 percent. Even highway departments are paying more attention to trees and shrubs to muffle roadway noise.

As you walk around your garden and home grounds, think fruitfully. Look at the sun that each area receives. Examine the soil to determine how you can improve it. Consider where some berry bushes might prosper. Multipurpose landscaping with berry bushes is the most tastefully rewarding way to enjoy the fruits of your gardening efforts.

Soil is alive. Even poor soils have their share of tiny organisms, helpful bacteria, and minute creatures at work underground. Every cubic foot of soil, depending on its fertility, can have millions of beneficial organisms with vital functions to perform. Some devour organic matter, helping to break it down and improve the structure of the soil. Others work on the soil itself, in cooperation with air and water, to break down minerals and other elements. Creatures such as earthworms burrow through the soil. As they digest organic material, they leave behind castings, providing a highly valuable nutrient for plant roots.

2

GOOD EARTH

BASICS

As organic matter is incorporated into the soil, it improves what is known as the *tilth*. Soil becomes more crumbly or, as scientists say, friable. Air and water and plant roots can move through soil better when it is in good condition.

Some gardens already have rich, deep, fertile topsoil. If your garden does, consider yourself especially lucky. A lot of land surrounding homes and developments, however, has just a light covering of topsoil added after construction. Sometimes the topsoil has been removed or turned under, and less desirable subsoil is on the top level. There are also natural variations in soil, such as sandy or heavy clay soils that are common to certain areas of the country. Don't fret. Whatever you have can be improved. Nature has been at work for centuries building and improving soils.

When you appreciate the good earth basics and know how to make soil come alive, you'll be well on your way to growing more productive, rewarding crops from your land, whatever its original condition. There are many simple steps you can take to improve certain conditions rapidly. Other steps will improve soil more slowly, year by year, until it becomes fertile and capable of producing better results than you thought possible.

MAKING COMPOST

Compost is one of the most useful materials you can make right in your own backyard to improve even good soils. Some people believe that compost is something used only by organic gardeners in their zeal to grow plants without artificial aids. That's just not so. Many of the so-called organic gardening techniques are well rooted in solid practicality. Long before chemical fertilizers were widely available to boost agricultural productivity, farmers relied on manure and other organic matter to improve their land.

Back on my family farm in New Jersey, we had compost piles working. I still rely on them on my farm in Maine. They provide that extra boost for lots of crops, from tomatoes to squash, and help get new fruit trees off to a favorable start.

You can make compost easily and without cost. All you need is a small spot to pile organic materials while they decompose into humus—or you can speed up the process.

THE LAYERING METHOD

■ The layering method is the easier of the two basic types of compost making, but it takes longer. To begin, you pick any convenient spot to pile organic matter. A spot out of sight is best, since a compost pile certainly isn't the most attractive part of a garden landscape.

All you do is pile old grass clippings, fallen leaves, and other organic materials from the garden—pruned softwood branches, debris from weeds, thinned plants—into a heap. You should start with about 4 to 6 inches of this type of material, then add a layer of soil about an inch thick. You can spread a pound of lime on the pile and a few inches of manure if it is available. If you don't have access to manure, you can spread a few cups of balanced garden fertilizer on the pile. Then add more layers of raked leaves, more clippings from the lawn, and organic debris from the kitchen, such as lettuce or cabbage leaves.

Don't use animal fats or bones, because they encourage pets and other animals to dig into the pile. Avoid using any diseased leaves. Weeds can be added, since the heat generated by the decaying vegetation effectively sterilizes most weed seeds.

In this layering process, anaerobic bacteria cause the decomposition. They work without the presence of air, but they do their work more slowly than do aerobic bacteria. Always leave a depression in the center of the compost pile. If you don't have rain regularly, keep the pile moist by periodic sprinkling with a hose, especially during dry periods. This moisture helps the rotting process.

Layering can be done along your berry bushes too. It takes time, but this practice can produce several benefits. Mulch layering—the simple and convenient process of spreading leaves, straw, grass clippings, and similar materials around your berry bushes and fruit trees—smothers weeds, retains soil moisture, and keeps soil cool in hot weather. In addition, the mulch gradually releases small quantities of nutrients into the soil as it slowly decays.

The fact is, composting solves the problem of disposing of leaves in the fall and grass clippings and plant prunings during the growing season. Many towns now ban the burning of leaves and brush, and it takes time and money to bag these materials and haul them away. You can even ask your neighbors for their leaves and clippings for your mulching and composting plans. If the neighbors don't want these materials, you both win.

THE INDORE METHOD

■The other compost method, known as the *Indore method*, gives you considerably faster results. It is based on the program developed in England many years ago by Sir Albert Howard, the father of modern organic gardening. You don't have to be an organic gardener to follow it. It pays to use the best of all different gardening techniques wherever they originate.

The Indore method has been revised in several ways over the years. All the variations involve turning the compost material periodically so that the fast-acting aerobic bacteria can decompose the material more quickly, since they work best in the presence of air. You can do the turning by pitchfork, by spade, or mechanically. By placing compost material into bins with perforated sides or providing wire frames through which air can move easily, you encourage this speedier decomposition.

The accompanying drawings show two of the easiest ways to build a simple backyard compost pile. In the first, tiles or cinder blocks are arranged to provide a three-sided bin.

In the second, a section of snow fence or wire fencing is used to create a sizable round bin. Regardless of how your compost bin is constructed, the process is the same: You pile all your

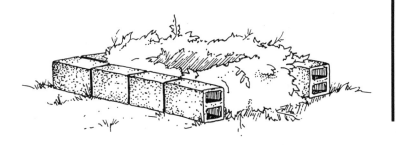

One easy way to begin backyard composting is with two rows of cinder blocks or tiles. Pile leaves, grass, clippings, and other organic matter between the rows and moisten and turn each week. Soon you'll have valuable humus for your garden.

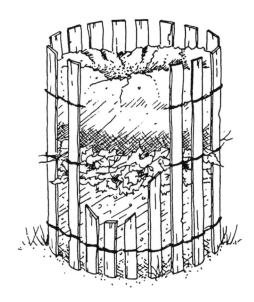

Another simple method is to use a roll of snow or wire fencing to contain all the organic matter you collect.

compostable material in the bin and then, once or twice a week (more often if you have time), you turn the material. Keep it moist so the anaerobic bacteria can also work.

Adding manure from cows, sheep, horses, or poultry incorporates nitrogen and small amounts of other nutrients. That's the preferred method of organic gardeners. You can add several cupfuls of 5-10-5 or 10-10-10 commercial fertilizer to help speed up the decay and incorporate those extra nutrients into the finished compost.

By following this regular aerating method, you'll get finished compost in two to three weeks if the moisture is adequate and the weather is warm. All types of compost activity slow down in dry or cold weather.

HOLE COMPOSTING
∾

From parts of Europe where topsoil is sparse and of poor quality, veteran fruit growers brought another soil-improvement tradition to America. They knew how to improve soil for fruit trees, grapevines, and other berry plants simply by making compost in a hole in the ground.

Consider the spots where you want to plant your bushes. Do they have sufficient sun but soil that isn't too promising? Well, dig into the ground. Make a hole at least twice the size of the normal spread of the roots of your intended plant. It is best to do this in the fall before planting. After your remove the soil, place leaves, manure, peat moss, grass clippings, and kitchen refuse into the hole. If the soil you removed is rocky but has a fair amount of organic matter and seems reasonably fertile, screen or pick out the rocks and other debris and mix the soil into the hole with the compost material. Add about a cup or two of fertilizer, depending on the size of the hole. Add an inch or so of topsoil to press down the lighter leaves and grass. Use a spading fork or spade to turn the material periodically, and remember to keep it moist.

If you have compost in a pit, you won't have unsightly piles around your yard. Aeration isn't perfect, but you'll be able to see how the material rots down into the hole. This porous, organically enriched base is excellent for encouraging root penetration, and it provides better drainage and moisture-holding capacity when you do the actual planting the following year.

Some years ago, one area of my garden in New Jersey had exceedingly poor soil and even worse subsoil. Much of it seemed to be typical Jersey red-shale soil. To improve the entire area quickly would have involved extensive work, so I tested this compost-hole system. It provided a wonderfully enriched base for a row of blackberry bushes. The next year, I made more holes. For several years I continued to improve the area, several compost holes at a time. By the end of four years, that entire berry area was thriving. During each year, I also mulched with as much straw, old hay, or leaves from fall raking as possible, up to 6 inches along rows and around bushes.

GREEN MANURE

If you have a chance to plan ahead for berry bushes, do so. Often a green manure crop of winter rye, clover, or similar plants can set deep roots that open the soil before you plant that berry patch or grape arbor. Legumes are best, especially clovers. They can fix nitrogen from the air on their root nodules. When you dig or till under these green manures, they release natural nitrogen freely to benefit the fruit crops you plant in that spot.

Interplanting also has its value. The first year, berries are usually slow to start. It may take several years for them to fill in an area such as a row or a hedge for a property border. In the meantime, the space shouldn't be wasted. You have a wide choice of other crops that can provide bountiful yields for one or two years between or in front of bushes until they fill in.

I favor cucumbers and squash. The vines creep along the ground, shading it and providing an interesting ground cover. Lettuce, broccoli, and even tomatoes are also suitable for interplanting. However, when you interplant, you must make allowances for the extra crops. They too need their own nutrients and moisture to reach prime maturity and begin setting crops. Soybeans and snap beans or limas work well. They take little space and, being legumes, they can also help improve the soil, contributing nitrogen from their roots for future use by trees and berry bushes.

PREPARING THE SOIL
∾

If you decide to set aside an area and improve it for berry bushes, here are some basic pointers. When you can, till the sod 8 to 18 inches deep. If there is no sod, you can start by spreading leaves, grass clippings, or similar material on the surface. When manure is available, spread a 1- or 2-inch layer on the ground. Dig or till it under, working it into the soil.

After the seedbed is raked smooth or tilled evenly, plant your winter cover crop of green manure. If your soil is reasonably fertile and you don't choose to plant green manure, you can prepare the soil either in the fall or just before spring planting. Some fruits do best when planted in spring, but you can do some fall planting if you do it early and well.

If you dig or till the selected site in the fall but choose to wait until spring to plant, spread some fertilizer on the surface in the fall. One pound of 10-10-10 or 10-6-4 per 20 square feet will work into the soil over the winter as moisture spreads through the soil. Most of it will still be there when needed at spring planting time, although some will have been used to help decompose organic material. A minor amount is also lost through leaching, especially in sandy soils.

Two other types of soil problems must also be addressed: how to deal with sandy soils and how to deal with clay soils.

Sandy soils tend to dry out. Many areas, especially coastal piedmont regions of the eastern states, have sandy soils. These don't hold moisture well. Neither do the sandy soils of the Southwest. In dry summers, shallow-rooted bushes can suffer badly in sandy soil. Fortunately, there are several easy ways to improve these soils quickly. Organic matter is the key, but you don't necessarily need compost. Peat moss is available from garden centers everywhere. It is one of the most versatile products to improve soils, especially sandy types. The best buys are the 6-cubic-foot bales.

Mix a bushel of peat moss to every estimated 2 bushels of sandy soil. Work it in well. Then, after planting, apply about 2 inches of peat as mulch. In the soil, peat improves the moisture-holding capacity of sandy soils. Applied to the surface, it retards evaporation and smothers weeds so they don't pull moisture from the soil to rob your plants of that vital element.

In soggier soils, those composed of large amounts of silt and clay particles, plants have another problem. Most plants, including berry bushes, can't stand wet feet. That's understandable when you realize that plant roots require air to breathe. Without air movement and adequate transfer of nutrients, as well as the ability of tiny feeding roots to penetrate soil, plants won't prosper. Clay soils in dry weather can form *hardpans*—compacted layers, often below the surface, that thwart root penetration. Sometimes you can see this problem right at the surface as the soil cracks in dry, hot weather. These soils may occur on just a portion of your property, usually in low-lying areas. Fortunately, you can change the soil texture and quality considerably. Here again, organic matter, especially peat, plays an important part.

Peat moss can be incorporated into clay-type soil, but don't do it when the ground is wet. Wait until the soil is somewhat dry, so digging or tilling won't compound the problem by forming clumps. Mixing sand and peat into clay soils is an excellent practice. Use one shovelful of sand and four to five shovelfuls of peat moss for each 2 to 4 square feet if the soil is heavy clay. Spread it on the surface and dig or till it in. After the first rain, check to determine how much you have improved the drainage. You may need to do this several years in a row to thoroughly improve the area.

Compost humus and manure can also be spread on clay soils. Each year you'll see improvement as you incorporate organic matter into the ground. Soggy soils are more difficult to improve than sandy ones, but you can succeed.

As you improve the soil, you'll notice that it physically comes alive. To prove this to yourself, dig a shovelful of soil near a compost pile or in an area that has been well mulched. You'll find little creatures, especially earthworms, at work. It is true that when you find lots of earthworms in soil, it is healthy.

Another fact about soil is abundantly true: In its natural state, it has a profile. This won't hold true if you are forced to garden on backfill around a home or building, but soil in natural areas forms in a systematic way. You can look for the profile in a desired planting area by digging down with a spade. If the land hasn't been touched much, you'll find a clearly visible profile with several horizons.

The upper level is the topsoil. It is a combination of the broken-down minerals and bits of gravel from the subsoil and the organic matter that has been dropped by living plants and decayed. Topsoil is usually darker than the next level below, which is the subsoil. The subsoil is also more gravelly than topsoil. Below this is the parent material, which may be anything from rocky soil to shale or bedrock, depending on where you live. The profile itself can be shallow, with just a bit of topsoil; or the profile can be deep, with rich layers of topsoil extending several feet down, as in the Great Plains areas.

Soil is formed slowly over tens of thousands of years. If you have good, deep soil, be thankful. But don't despair if your home isn't blessed with good topsoil. All soil can be improved, but a warning is in order. Although it may seem logical to improve a garden area for berries and even vegetable and flower gardens by purchasing topsoil, it pays to have the topsoil tested before you buy it, to be sure it has a reasonable fertility and isn't merely fill.

SOIL FACTS
ᐁ

Several other facts about your soil should be considered as you begin your fruitful landscape plantings. First, learn about the types of soils.

TEXTURE refers to the size of the majority of the particles making up the soil. They can range from tiny, almost microscopic, clay particles to small stones or gravel.

CLAY soils can be stony clay, gravelly or sandy clay, silty clay, or just plain muddy clay.

Loamy soils may be coarse, medium, fine, sandy, silty, or clay loams.

Sandy soils can be gravelly, coarse, medium, fine, or loamy.

These are the terms that your county agent may use when helping you to evaluate your sites and planting areas.

Structure of soil is determined by the way in which individual particles are grouped. A good soil structure lets plant roots, air, and water move freely through it. Loamy and clay soils may have a crumbly structure. Sandy soils have little granulation. Clay soils compact readily.

The easiest way to evaluate soil structure is this: Pick up a handful at planting time and make a fist. If it crumbles easily after you have squeezed it in your fist, the soil is probably the desirable sandy loam. The closer you can get to a granular feel with clusters of soil that easily shake apart, the better. Organic matter—peat, compost, and humus—will keep you on track in your soil-improvement plan.

One final point should be understood as you select your planting sites and go about whatever soil-improvement program needed to make your land more productive. Three kinds of water are found in any type of soil:

1. Gravitational water. In sandy soils, water often drains out too quickly, leaving plants to wilt or perform poorly. In clay soils, gravitational water lingers longer to create soggy spots. Soil pores get clogged with water, which can rot roots.

2. Hygroscopic soil water. This water is chemically bound with soil materials. It is basically unavailable to plants, so it's of no great concern to you.

3. Capillary water. This is the most important soil moisture. It is free to leave the soil and enter growing roots. As it does, it carries plant food up through the stems or trunks into branches, twigs, and leaves. This water is most available when soil texture and structure are crumbly and loamy, with ample organic matter incorporated into the soil.

Entire books have been written about soil. This chapter is meant as a primer. The good earth may be awaiting your planting of fruitful trees and bushes now. If not, heed the hints of this chapter and improve it. Soil is truly alive and can become more alive and healthier—with your help.

One of the important things I learned from giving gardening tips on TV is the need for brevity. Here are some simple, down-to-earth guidelines for selecting, planting, and tending berry bushes. Other details are provided in the chapters on the different berry bushes, but for easy reference, this list is handy. My thanks to the fine people at the New York State Fruit Testing Cooperative for suggesting these guide-lines, which are based on their exceptional knowledge of fruit planting.

FRUITFUL

PLANTING

GUIDELINES

PLANTING TIPS AND CULTURE GUIDE

1. Everything begins in the soil. Most berry bushes thrive in deep, well-drained, and friable (crumbly) soils. Currants and gooseberries do well in heavy soils, but strawberries prefer a lighter soil, a sandy loam.

2. Age of plants is important. The youngest usually transplant the best and are the least expensive.

3. Planting time varies for different types. Small fruits can be planted in spring or fall, but spring is recommended by most experts. Plant in early spring so plants get a good start and have extra growing time during good weather.

Many varieties of berries cannot survive in northern areas where winter temperatures can drop to -30°F or lower. Plant breeders have been working on this problem and home gardeners now have a choice of plump, tasty berries on hardy plants that can survive even in states and areas with prolonged sub-zero winter climates.

Plant Hardiness Zones, also called Horticultural Zones, have been identified and mapped by the U. S. Department of Agriculture. Your County Agricultural Extension Agent or State Agricultural College can provide you with details about the Horticultural Zones in your state.

It helps to have a basic understanding of these zones, because you'll find that nurseries and mail-order plant catalogs usually tell you which plants fall into which zones.

Zones are divided by approximate range of *average annual minimum* temperatures for each zone.

Zone 1	Below −50 degrees F
Zone 2	−50 to −40 degrees F
Zone 3	−40 to −30 degrees F
Zone 4	−30 to −20 degrees F
Zone 5	−20 to −10 degrees F
Zone 6	−10 to 0 degrees F
Zone 7	0 to +10 degrees F
Zone 8	+10 to +20 degrees F
Zone 9	+20 to +30 degrees F
Zone 10	+30 to +40 degrees F

4. Selecting the right site is important. Plant where you like for eye appeal, convenience, and other personal considerations, provided the soil is good. If it isn't, improve it. Avoid frost pockets and low areas where frost settles, and be sure that your site is blessed with ample sun.

5. Pollination is necessary. Without it, fruit set is reduced or doesn't occur. It is good insurance to have at least two compatible varieties that pollinate each other in the same vicinity. Most berries pollinate themselves.

6. Variety selection is up to you, but look through your catalogs carefully. Some old and new varieties offer special advantages, from great taste to disease resistance. Some varieties are better for all purposes than others; some are good for either freezing or fresh use but are not good for both.

7. Consider multiple values. Blackberries, raspberries, grapes, blueberries, and elderberries all make attractive hedges that you can eat. Currants, gooseberries, and blueberries are well suited for borders or can be interplanted with other shrubs and trees.

8. Bear with your trees and shrubs. They'll bear well for you when you plant and tend them properly. Small fruits begin bearing within two to three years, depending on when you plant them and on the growing conditions. Grapes take three to four years before they begin rewarding you with fruit. Remember, to stretch your harvest season, select *early-, mid-, and late-bearing* varieties. Charts on bearing age, productive capacity, and other helpful information are usually included in mail-order catalogs.

9. Planting is easy, but don't rush through it. Open your plants when they arrive. If you can't plant them immediately, make sure the roots are tucked safely beneath moist soil in a shady spot. If the roots have dried, soak them in a mixture of compost and water—one cup per gallon—as a slurry. Always keep roots from drying in the sun while planting.

Be sure to dig the hole large enough to give roots space to spread naturally. Restricted planting slows growth and may delay your harvest by a year or more. Before planting, prune damaged parts and broken root tips. Pack the soil firmly and water well. Bush fruits should usually be planted the same depth as or slightly deeper than they were in the nursery. See the appropriate chapters for details on specific fruit.

10. After proper planting, pruning is perhaps the single most important factor in producing an abundance of fruit. It stimulates the growth of shoots, branches, and canes, resulting in a new fruiting wood. Make pruning cuts to an outside bud so new branches grow out, not into the center. The better you prune, the more success you'll have with fruit plants.

11. Mulch is a boon for good gardening. Collect old leaves, grass clippings, straw, and similar organic materials. Use them as mulch or compost them and use the compost as mulch. Mulch saves moisture, smothers weeds, keeps fruit bushes tidier, and adds minute amounts of nutrients.

12. Feed your plants if you expect them to feed you. Nitrogen is the most important element, but a balance of all the essential nutrients is important for berries. For the most abundant crops, year after year, you must put back into the soil what your growing crops take out.

13. Pests play a part in every effort to grow bushes or plants. Insects and diseases can thwart your best efforts. Plant breeders have built disease-resistance into improved varieties, and new and improved pesticides are safer to use and can help you conquer even the most stubborn problems. Play it safe and always doublecheck the manufacturer's directions. Be careful while mixing and applying, and always keep chemicals away from youngsters.

14. Know how to tell when fruit is ripe. Details are included in the chapters on individual fruits.

If you want to enjoy one of the tastiest fruit berries and have a handsome hedge that grows even in poor-quality soil, think blackberries. Blackberries are seldom sold in supermarkets or local stores, but occasionally you'll find them offered at country fruit stands. These are not the smallish, overtart berries found in bramble patches along country lanes. These blackberries are plump, juicy, and prolific. From just two rows along one field, I harvested more than 300 quarts the third year after planting.

4

BLACKBERRIES

If you prefer to avoid the bramble thorns that catch on clothes, new thornless blackberry varieties are available. They're also productive, vigorous, and winter-hardy as far north as Illinois, Ohio, and New Jersey. Other types, with their typical thorns, thrive much farther north.

Few fruits for the home ground are as dependable in production as blackberries. They prefer temperate climates, so they're not as well adapted to the Plains states or mountain areas, but they're worth a try in most other areas. Once established, blackberries will produce crops for fifteen to twenty years. That's surprising longevity.

Almost any type of soil is suitable for blackberries, provided they can get (or you can provide) ample moisture come fruiting time. They do best, however, in sandy loams, since their roots may penetrate 2 to 3 feet deep. Clay soils may restrict this natural growth and, consequently, the yield. Where shelter from harsh winter winds is possible, give them that advantage. Some varieties can take more cold than others, but if you have a wind-break of a house, garage, or tree, blackberries appreciate this consideration. As with all fruits, avoid frost pockets or areas where water stands in winter. Blackberries also appreciate lots of sun, but they can produce reasonably well in areas that are not suited for other berry bushes or fruit trees. Put their more toler-ant growing abilities to work on some of these neglected areas.

You can select either the upright types or trailing varieties.

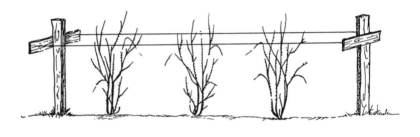

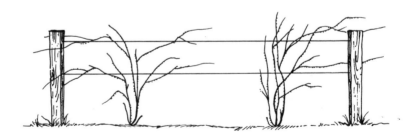

The two best ways to train and control blackberries are: A—using two parallel wires to contain the plants, and B—using one wire above the other.

The upright ones are superior. They are more productive, respond well to cultivation, and produce vigorous growth and bountiful harvests. Typical growth is similar to that of their wild relatives. The erect bushes have arched, self-supporting canes. You can train them to arbors much as you would train grapevines. Several other systems work well. You can allow them to spread into a thick hedge to border a backyard. They can be guided to grow upright between two horizontal wires strung side by side between posts or beside two horizontal wires strung one above the other between posts.

VARIETIES
∾

With the renewed interest in blackberries, nurseries are offering several excellent, taste-tempting varieties. Thanks to the skill of plant breeders, these berries are much bigger than wild ones. Since the erect varieties are so much easier to tend and perform so much better, I've concentrated only on them in this chapter. Trailing types, more commonly called dewberries, are included in Chapter 6.

LAWTON is widely grown for its medium, sweet fruit. It is restricted to southern areas.

RAVEN has medium-large berries that are medium-firm; eating quality is excellent. Plants are moderately vigorous and productive.

RANGER is similar to Raven but more adapted to Atlantic coastal areas.

SMOOTHSTEM is one of the first thornless varieties. Fruit is medium to large, firm, and tart. It is a semiupright variety and can be grown on a trellis, but it may suffer in hot, dry, windy areas.

CHEROKEE is a 1974 introduction from the University of

Arkansas. The firm fruit is medium to large and grows on vigorous, erect canes.

BLOWERS is a good midseason berry of dessert quality. It has large, firm berries on hardy, vigorous bushes and ripens over a long season.

EARLY HARVEST has medium-size, firm berries on moderately vigorous bushes. It is better suited to southern areas but is very productive as far north as Maryland and southern Illinois.

JERSEYBLACK is an early, long-season variety with medium to large berries. Bushes are semitrailing and need some support.

ALFRED was developed in Michigan. It is early and has large, firm, sweet berries on vigorous, productive bushes. It is adapted to northern areas with climate's similar to Michigan's .

DARROW is the standout among blackberries. It is so superior to all other varieties that some nurseries have dropped other types in favor of Darrow. It is particularly noteworthy for its vigor, reliably heavy production, firmness, and quality. Plants are hardier than many other types, making Darrow a good choice for gardeners in northern states. Berries may be an inch or more long and three-quarters of an inch wide and are glossy black. Another advantage is the long harvest season. You may need to pick berries several times, since Darrow continues yielding for weeks. The fruit is good fresh, for pies or freezing, or for blackberry wine. With good fertilization, Darrow forms such a thick hedge that it kept some wandering ponies from galloping across my gardens.

DIRKSEN THORNLESS and **BLACK SATIN** are two varieties originated by the U.S. Agricultural Research Service in cooperation with Southern Illinois University. Both are thornless, productive, and vigorous, but they aren't very hardy in northern areas.

HIMALAYAN GIANT was developed by Dutch experiment station specialists. This blackberry bush produces fruit an inch and a quarter in diameter and weighing 10 grams (.35 oz.) each. In trials, three-year-old plants produced 50 to 60 pounds per bush. It is hardy to zone 2.

HERITAGE SELECT is another hardy blackberry shrub that produces large, glossy black fruit that is excellent for pies, jams, and eating fresh. It is hardy to zone 3.

STARK JUMBO BLACKBERRY is a Shawnee cultivar that produces colossal, plump blackberries and large crops. Berries often grow to an inch and a half long. These plants bear and ripen over a longer time than many others.

CHOCTAW blackberries (a patented variety) are glossy and flavorful. They usually ripen right at the end of the strawberry season. They are easy to pick on erect plants.

PLANTING POINTERS

Nurseries may sell rooted cuttings of erect-type blackberries. These are 4 to 6 inches long, about one-eighth to one-quarter inch in diameter. They don't look like much, but they can surprise you. The more vigorous rooted suckers, 12 to 15 inches long, are a better bet, however. They are stronger, take root faster, and begin to send out their own underground suckers the second year to fill in the rows.

Prepare the soil thoroughly. Although blackberries will perform in poor soil, they welcome additions of organic matter. Manure, if available, can be tilled into the soil the fall before you plant. That preparation helps set the stage for future prosperity. Since blackberry plants establish deep roots, digging or tilling 8 to 12 inches deep is worthwhile. If the soil tends to be heavy, you can prepare slight ridges to receive the plants. That way, excess moisture drains away but is available for feeder roots as the bushes mature into hedges.

You can plant blackberries anytime during the dormant season, but early spring is best. That way, you won't shock tender varieties if the winter is especially severe that first year.

Blackberries need somewhat more room to ramble into natural brambles than do other types of berries. Blackberries are also noted for propagating themselves quite rapidly with underground runners or suckers.

If you have wild blackberry bushes on your property, try to eliminate them before you introduce cultivated varieties. While these native wild ones may be resistant to diseases they may also harbor some infections that can be transmitted to domesticated varieties. That's a good approach with other fruit crops too.

If you can't plant immediately, heel the rootstocks into the soil as you would other trees or bushes and keep the roots moist. One year I lost a fair number of plants because they dried out in the sun. To avoid that hazard while planting, keep moist burlap over the roots. Better yet, keep the plants in a bucket of water with moist burlap over the canes. They may be somewhat sensitive as you plant them, but once the plants are established, they'll be with you for years to come.

If you are planting the small root pieces 4 to 6 inches long, set them about 6 inches apart along the row. If you are planting rootstocks that are 12 to 18 inches tall, set them 3 to 4 feet apart in rows. If you prefer parallel rows, keep the rows 6 to 8 feet apart. Blackberry plants will spread along the row and fill it in, but you need room between rows to tend them.

Set plants the same depth at which they grew in the nursery. You can see that point on the canes, just above where the roots have formed. Tamp the soil around rootstocks well to establish firm contact with the soil, then water. A good soaking is helpful at this point and again each week until the plants are well started.

If you desire just a clump or grouping in a corner, you can space the plants 3 to 4 feet apart. They'll fill in well in later years. Judicious pruning will let you walk among them for harvesting. For the most effective use of superior varieties such as Darrow, hedgerow planting is recommended. It costs a bit more to space plants closer, but you'll find that they fill in more rapidly, especially if mulched with straw and manure and fertilized each season.

After planting and watering blackberry plants, take your pruning shears and cut the plants back to half the height from the ground. This encourages the desired side growth of lateral branches.

FEEDING
∾

Mulching blackberries with compost, straw, grass clippings, and similar materials is better than clean cultivation. If you don't have enough mulch, carefully cultivate around the bushes just a bit to remove grass and weeds. Blackberries are shallow rooted; you shouldn't disturb them as they set their first year's vital root structure.

Although blackberries can thrive in poor soils, they respond quite vigorously to soil improvement with organic material. If you can provide a winter cover mulch the first year, do so. That first season is the toughest on the plants until they are more deeply rooted.

For maximum yields, apply fertilizer every year at blossoming time. The year I used several inches of stable manure was the best one ever. Unfortunately, manure may not be available. If not, apply a commercial 5-10-5 fertilizer as a top dressing along the rows each year when they bloom. Spread an average of 1 cup per parent plant along the rows—half a cup on each side—and water after you apply it. Figure on 5 to 10 pounds of 5-10-5 per 100 feet of row, depending on the maturity and density of the rows.

Judging from split fertilizing trails I've seen, I believe that it pays to apply half the fertilizer just before blossom time to get canes and new fruiting wood in prime condition. Then apply the second half within several weeks as tiny fruits are forming. As soon as fruits form, pay more attention to watering. Blackberries need copious amounts of moisture to produce their plumpest, sweetest fruit for you.

PRUNING
∾

If you wish to control blackberry bushes, pruning is necessary. If you want a bramble patch that is closer to the natural state, periodic trimming to let you walk among the plants is satisfactory. Blackberries astound most home gardeners with their constant spreading habit.

Crowns of blackberry plants are perennial; new canes arise from them each year. The canes, however, are biennial; they live only two years. During the first year after planting, let your plants bush out. The second year, you'll find new suckers filling in the open spots and new canes sprouting from the crowns and around them.

During the first two years, blackberry canes send out laterals, also called side branches. The second year, small branches grow from buds on these laterals. This is the fruiting wood. After the laterals fruit, these canes die. That makes pruning a simple procedure.

Prune laterals back each spring after the second year. Before growth starts, cut laterals to about 12 inches long. Check the ground area for new sucker canes arising. If you let them all grow, your bushes will turn into a matted thicket. During each growing season, remove all suckers that arise between rows or too far from the primary area. Use heavy gloves and pull up these out-of-place suckers. If you merely cut them, they often regrow.

Come summer, when your harvest is over, cut out the old canes. They're easy to distinguish—in both size and color—from the new wood, which will produce next year's fruit. If too many new canes have grown, thin them, leaving four to six per bush. It pays to burn old canes in order to kill diseases. Anthracnose and rosette can be problems, particularly in southern regions. Burning eliminates this threat, since diseases overwinter mainly on old wood.

After you've removed old canes, trim lateral branches back as you did the year before to about 12 inches in length. The number of canes per foot of row may vary according to variety, but practice will guide you year to year.

Blackberries can become exceedingly tall if not trimmed back in fall or winter. Whether you wish a bramble hedge or not, remember that pruning encourages greater yields. When erect blackberry plants reach 30 to 40 inches tall, cut off their top tips. This pruning forces canes to branch. Tipped canes also grow stouter, making them better able to support heavier fruit crops. You can sacrifice some yield by letting canes grow thick, but when they are overdense, yield suffers.

If you prefer a trellis pattern for a more decorative effect, you can tie canes in bundles and then attach them with stout cord to the desired wire, wood, or fence supports. A two-wire trellis will neatly hold your taller canes and keep them from drooping. In spring you can easily place those that are out of position within the desired guidelines. This support also helps keep your crop at a handier picking level.

HARVESTING
∾

Blackberries received their name on purpose. We may be tempted to pick them as soon as they seem plump and dark, but just a few tastes will correct that error. As fruits mature, they become more intensely blue-black, increase in size, and become less firm. As they seem to be ripening, pluck a few. You'll soon be able to tell when they're fully ripe. Look them over every day or so and pick the ripe ones. It is best to harvest blackberries early in the day. They won't spoil as rapidly if picked when it is relatively cool.

PROPAGATING
∾

Blackberries provide dozens upon dozens of new sucker shoots each year, and you can profit from this habit. Just dig up the sucker plants that are about 12 to 18 inches tall—root and all. Keep them moist and cool until they can be replanted. You can encourage even faster reproduction in your own garden rows by bending the tips of the tallest canes to the ground and covering each with a shovelful of soil. Do this after summer harvest, right through the fall, and by next spring, those canes will be rooted. Just separate them from the parent, dig up the roots, and you'll have new plants to use as you wish.

Blueberry bushes in the wild have two distinctive shapes: highbush and lowbush. The lowbush kind is difficult if not impossible to cultivate and doesn't yield anywhere near the amount you can get from the prolific highbush blueberries. A walk in the woods along swampy areas may yield a basket or two of lowbush berries, but for practical purposes around your home, highbush berries are your best bet.

Blueberries are one fruit crop that can give you the greatest pleasure and the most fruit for the least effort in your backyard fruit garden. They provide pleasure in three ways:

1. They make good ornamental shrubs.

2. They're a productive source of food.

3. They're attractive to songbirds. This may prove to be more of a minus than a plus, however, unless you protect your crop with special netting.

Blueberries are somewhat different in their soil needs from other fruit bushes. Blueberries prefer soil that is loose, well aerated, and acid, with a pH of about 4.8 to 5.0 for best results. The pH is a gauge that tells whether soil is acid, neutral, or alkaline. Lower numbers indicate an acid condition. Numbers from 6.0 to 7.5 indicate neutral or so-called sweeter soil, and higher numbers (8 to 9) indicate alkaline conditions. Simple soil tests by your county agent or local garden center or with a home soil-test kit can tell you where your soil ranks on the pH scale.

Most homeowners who live east of the Mississippi, where blueberries are native, know that their soil tends to be on the acid side naturally. Others can make their soil more acid in several simple ways. The addition of oak and maple leaves and pine or evergreen needles, dug or tilled under, tends to acidify soil. Adding nitrogen fertilizer also helps. Wood chips and pine bark also build up the acid level. For soil that is extremely acid already, lime neutralizes acidity and sweetens the soil.

Blueberries are different from most berry bushes in another unusual way. The blueberry root has no root hairs, as do many other plants. However, the entire root system is very fine, fibrous, and hairlike in structure. Such fine hairs can't push their way through heavy clay-type soils. When you see blueberries in the wild, you'll notice that they thrive in highly organic sandy soil near streams and around ponds. That's important to know as you select your planting site or begin improving the soil that will support your blueberry bushes.

Blueberries also need lots of water. However, they can't abide wet feet, since constant water in the soil clogs air space and rots their roots. That's true for most plants, but especially true for blueberries. Because they are very shallow rooted and have such a fine root structure, blueberries must have adequate moisture at all times, especially during fruiting.

VARIETIES

Blueberry varieties are available to fit your climate. In northern areas, the *Vaccinium corymbosum*, *Vaccinium australe*, and hybrids developed from these types are quite hardy. They thrive from the Carolinas to Michigan and Maine. In southern areas, another group descended from *Vaccinium ashei* has been improved upon by plant breeders. It is a highbush type better known as rabbit-eye blueberry across the South from Florida to Texas. These plants can soar to 10 feet tall but are kept manageable by pruning. The northern types are usually 3 to 6 feet tall. These too need pruning to maintain their shape and promote more abundant bearing.

Most northern varieties are considered self-fruitful, but it pays to grow several varieties together. This provides better cross-pollination, resulting in larger and more numerous berries. If you want early, midseason, and late varieties to extend your harvest, be sure to choose varieties that overlap in blooming to get the best possible pollination. If you have the space and you delight in blueberry pies, plant a selection.

EARLIBLUE is an early type that is upright, spreading, and vigorous. It produces medium loose clusters of large, firm blueberries.

COLLINS is similar to Earliblue but ripens a bit later.

WEYMOUTH is a smaller, more open, and spreading bush. It can fit neatly in border areas around your home. It too is an early type, but its quality is not as good as that of the others.

STANLEY is a midseason type that is erect and vigorous. Fruits are medium loose with firm and aromatic berries that taste great.

BLUERAY is an upright, vigorous, and somewhat spreading, midseason variety. Fruit clusters are small and tight, but berries are very large, light blue, and firm. Blueray is one of the best for dessert use.

BLUECROP is a vigorous bush, upright in growth, and nicely productive in midseason. Fruit clusters are loose with large, light blue, firm, and aromatic berries, but the quality is not as good as that of Blueray.

HERBERT is vigorous, open, and productive among the late-ripening varieties. It has large to medium berries of good eating quality.

CORVILLE is also a vigorous, spreading, and productive late type. It bears large to medium-size berries that are firm, tart, and good for eating.

BLUEBERRY NORTH-SKY is perhaps the hardiest of all named varieties. When planted in well-drained, acidic soil, this variety produces an abundance of medium-size, light-blue berries with a wild blueberry flavor. It is a tree-type plant that grows to 10 feet tall and spreads 2 to 3 feet in diameter.

RABBIT-EYE blueberries, the typical southern name for these highbush beauties, are not very self-fruitful. Therefore, it is always best to plant several different types so that the period of bloom overlaps, ensuring adequate cross-pollination.

In southern areas, attention has been focused on developing improved varieties that fit the climate conditions of warmer areas. The University of Georgia has been active in developing well-suited new blueberries. Several thousand seedlings have been grown over the past decade. Three show exceptional results:

SOUTHLAND is moderately vigorous and produces a dense and compact plant, unlike some of its parents, which were too tall for convenient home garden use. Berries are light blue, medium-large, and firm, with good flavor. Southland blooms at the same time as Tiftblue, ensuring better pollination if you plant both varieties together.

BRITEBLUE results from a cross between a native blueberry called Ethel and a Georgia variety, Callaway. They cross-produce an open plant with firm berries that are ready in midseason.

DELITE is an upright plant with numerous branches. It bears large, round, light-blue berries with excellent flavor. Berries ripen late compared with other, older varieties, and they keep well on the plant if you can't pick them right away.

Other good southern varieties include **CALLAWAY, COASTAL, HOME-BELL, TIFTBLUE,** and **WOODARD.**

Now that blueberries are gaining popularity in home gardens, alert nurseries are providing a larger range of varieties for your selection. In fact, experimenters at the University of Minnesota have been working on exceptionally winter-hardy blueberry varieties. They must do so if they hope to develop bushes that will survive in that extreme winter weather. Their efforts have been directed toward crossing low-growing native blueberry bushes of Minnesota with more desirable varieties. The objective is tastier berries on bushes that can withstand temperatures of −25°F and colder. The experimenters have noted that the low-growing varieties fit nicely into home landscape plans and survive under deep snow cover better than do taller bushes.

PLANTING POINTERS

If your chosen site needs more organic matter, start improving the soil at least a year before planting. Blueberries get off to a strong start when the area is well prepared. Avoid sod areas if possible, and add manure, straw, peat moss, compost—the more organic material the better. You can provide more in the future with mulches that rot down bit by bit.

Add pine bark, pine needles, and oak leaves if they are available. Let the material decompose naturally, just as you would in the natural layering method of making compost. In fact, consider your blueberry area a compost bed. The fall before you plan to plant blueberries, till or dig the organic material under. It will rot even more as it becomes part of your improved soil mixture for your new plants.

Another reason to prepare the soil for them a year in advance is to eliminate persistent weeds such as Bermuda grass in the South and nutgrass and other pesky weeds in more northern areas. Weeds rob soils of an amazing amount of water and nutrients. Weeds must be banished by removing them or smothering them with mulch.

Natural soils in commercial blueberry-growing areas of New Jersey, Wisconsin, Rhode Island, Michigan, and parts of the South from Alabama to Texas have a naturally high water table. Water is seldom more than 12 to 18 inches below the surface. That's a key to good blueberry culture. If you don't have a high water table, keep in mind that consistent mulching and watering will be necessary for optimum blueberry production. That's easy to do with a soaker hose attached to a timer. You turn it on each morning and it shuts off automatically after giving your blueberries their necessary drink. The mulch prevents the water from evaporating.

Blueberries may all look alike in stores, but for your home plantings you have a selection of tasty varieties. Some are ideal for fresh use; others are better for pies, jams, and preserves. Some are multipurpose. You can get year-old stock, but nurseries often offer two- and three-year-old plants as well. Blueberries sold as one-year-old plants normally are rooted cuttings direct from the propagating bed or tray. Their roots may not be developed well enough to withstand any setbacks at planting or during their first year if drought occurs or the winter is particularly severe. Two-year-old plants are rooted cuttings that normally have spent a year in the ground at the nursery. They are better prepared for transplanting into a new location. There is little value in buying older plants. They cost more, but they usually mature no more rapidly than two-year-olds that get a firm foothold in your soil.

If you buy mail-order plants, be certain to emphasize where you live. In the rush of a busy season, clerks may not notice that you need warm-weather or cold-weather varieties. Mark your order form clearly so that the nursery can send you the right type for your area. Reliable nurseries often suggest that you change a selection if you believe that you have picked one that won't prosper in your locale.

The best planting time is early in spring, as soon as the soil can be worked without becoming cloddy and lumpy from excess moisture. Space your plants so that they'll have room to grow to their fullest size for maximum yields. Set plants about 4 feet apart in rows. If you want a hedgerow effect, they can be set closer. Remember, however, that if you do this, you'll need to pay closer attention to providing fertilizer and moisture. When you plant in several rows, leave enough room to walk easily among your bushes at harvest time. A 5-foot-diameter circle is usually sufficient.

Blueberry bushes can also be interplanted among your azaleas, rhododendrons, and various pine, fir, or spruce shrubs. As long as they have the acid soil that they love, they can be mixed and matched with evergreens to add appeal to your conventional landscape shrubbery.

For each new plant, dig an area about 2 feet in diameter and 6 inches deep. That may sound like a rather large area for such a small bush, but these are very shallow-rooted plants. The hairlike roots will spread at or close to the soil surface. That extra pulverizing of the soil around them when planting helps the roots take hold. Mixing peat moss in to make the surface soil a mixture of one-half peat moss and one-half soil also helps plants get the strongest start possible.

Fall planting is possible with two- or three-year-old plants, but be sure to prepare the soil well and mulch the plants. Spread sawdust 4 to 6 inches deep around fall-planted blueberry plants. Peat, straw, or other materials are good, but sawdust improves and maintains that vital soil acidity. It also conserves moisture, smothers weeds that might rob your plants of nutrients, and prevents excessive freezing and thawing of the ground, which can break roots. This extra fall application of mulch helps insulate the plants during their first winter.

Whenever you plant blueberries, always keep their fragile root structure moist. Don't tamp the soil as you would for most other plants. Pat it into place, leaving it fairly loose. Those fine roots need all the help they can get to penetrate the soil around the bush.

FEEDING
∾

Nitrogen is the main fertilizer element needed by blueberries. Don't add any the first year if you planted one-year-old stocks. Blueberry plants grow in what is known as *flushes*: one early in the spring—followed by a pause—and another a month or so later. Use a garden fertilizer such as 10-10-10 or 10-6-4, applying about a quarter of a pound around each two-year-old plant. Spread fertilizer on the soil or on top of the mulch over the entire root zone—the area extending out from the plant to the drip line, which is the farthest reach of the branches.

Since nitrogen is the key element, you should use the more readily available forms, especially if sawdust, wood chips, or bark is used as mulch. These cellulose materials also need nitrogen to continue their own decomposition process, so they may take it from the soil, reducing the amount available to your plants.

Using a quarter of a cup of ammonium nitrate around each bush is recommended in spring. When blueberries are mulched, spread a quarter of a pound of ammonium sulfate, or its equivalent, each spring when buds begin to swell. A second application can be made about 6 weeks later. As plants become fully mature and bear 3 to 4 quarts of berries each, you can increase this amount a bit.

It's a good idea to mulch blueberries continually. Each spring and fall, add more. With all this emphasis on mulching, it may seem as though you are being asked to do extra work. Not so. Mulching—that simple spreading of peat, compost, leaves, or sawdust—takes only a few minutes per plant. It saves you hours of weeding and cultivating and helps you avoid damage to plants. In addition, your plants—and subsequently you—gain the benefits of higher yields.

PRUNING

After planting, remove all fruit buds from the young plants. You want the first year's strength to go into root and branch growth rather than a feeble attempt to set a few berries.

Prune away any dead or damaged wood and short twigs. Fruiting shoots that will bear next year's crop should be about the length of a lead pencil, coming from the branches on one-year-old plants. Round, fat fruit buds will grow on the tips of these shoots to bloom next season. Each fruit bud will produce a cluster of berries.

It is important that sufficient pruning be done each year to

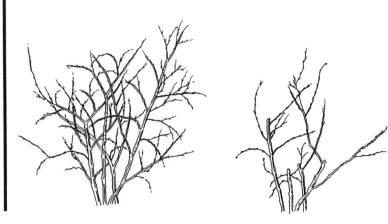

When a blueberry bush is overgrown, like the one on the left, it won't be as productive as it should be. Prune your blueberry bush to encourage new, young, and more productive wood, as shown on the right.

maintain bush vigor and encourage production of a number of strong fruiting shoots each year. Prune with two purposes in mind: to adjust the fruit crop to the capacity of the bush and its root system, and to stimulate strong, vigorous shoots to produce next year's crop. If the bush is overloaded with fruit one year, there will be little strength left in the plant to produce enough vegetative growth for future years. Subsequent crops will be fewer, and the bush will become weak and twiggy with small fruit.

Blueberry bushes send up new shoots each year. These can be headed back to encourage side laterals that will bear large fruit. The best pruning time is early spring. You can identify fruit buds by their large size and estimate your potential crop. Remove sucker shoots and all weak, twiggy branches that are small and spindly. Thin the vigorous fruiting wood to one or two fruit buds per 3 to 4 inches of shoot growth. Keep in mind that each fruit bud will produce at least six to eight berries.

Limit the number of canes or main branches rising near the crown to one or two for each year of age of the plant. An alternative guide is to limit the canes or main branches from the crown to one or two for each foot of height of the bush. That should leave a maximum of six to ten canes for older, mature bushes.

As your blueberry bushes mature year by year, vigorous new canes will rise from the crown and may tower over the average height of your bush. Simply head them back to the average size of the plant. Remove older, weaker ones. That way, your blueberry bushes will automatically replenish themselves with strong, vigorous new growth over the years.

In time you'll be able to remove some of the older, lower branches. That will let the taller, more vigorous ones with their laterals produce a more convenient, more productive plant in the years ahead. And you won't have to stoop to pick the berries.

HARVESTING
☙

Most blueberry varieties ripen over a period of several weeks. Be prepared to pick your berries several times. They should be fully colored and pop easily from the cluster. Berries usually turn blue several days before they develop their maximum sweetness and flavor. Gently roll them from the cluster with your thumb into the palm of your hand. Those berries that are not quite ripe usually remain attached to the stem for picking later. With practice, you'll get the feel of this simple process. Avoid overhandling berries, because you'll rub the typical "bloom" from the fruit. Its removal does no harm but reduces their eye appeal.

Plant some blueberries this season. In a year or two, with little care other than mulching, pruning, and fertilizing—which amounts to an hour's work per bush per year—you'll have berries aplenty.

In England, currants and other old-fashioned fruits are commonly grown, but these delicious and easy-to-grow fruits have never really taken root in America. Many of these less-known fruits can be a colorful addition to home landscapes. They take little room, and some can be trained on posts or fences. Others sparkle with blooms and fruit as interplanted bushes among other shrubs and trees.

6

CURRANTS,

GOOSEBERRIES,

ELDERBERRIES,

AND

DEWBERRIES

CURRANTS AND GOOSEBERRIES

Currants and gooseberries are used mainly in making jellies, jams, preserves, and pies. Red gooseberries are sweet when fully ripe and may be eaten fresh. Currants can also be eaten fresh, but they may be too tart for you.

The home growing of currants and gooseberries has been restricted because of certain insects and diseases associated with them. Federal and state regulations prohibited the growing of these plants in certain states. The purpose of these restrictions was to prevent the transmittal of any exotic plant pests or diseases that might threaten other major commercial crops.

Fortunately, because of new varieties, clean rootstocks, and improved materials to fight insects and fungus diseases, currants, gooseberries, and other unusual fruits can now be grown widely. Restrictions still exist in some areas, however, so you may want to check with your county agricultural agent or state college of agriculture about the situation in your area. (A list of state agricultural colleges is included in the appendices.)

Although you can buy healthy currant and gooseberry plants, they may serve as host to white pine blister rust disease. Therefore, some states require a permit to grow currants and gooseberries and won't issue one if you live within 1,500 feet of sizable ornamental or commercial white pine stands. To be a good gardening neighbor, check on the restrictions in your area. You don't want to encourage problems in nearby woodlands.

CURRANT VARIETIES

WILDER is one of the best currant varieties. It has large, dark-red, subacid berries that hang in large, compact clusters. The bush is upright and may grow 4 feet tall or more without pruning, but it is easy to pick and vigorous.

RED LAKE ripens after Wilder. It has large, firm, lighter red berries. Clusters are large and hang on long after ripening. It is upright, vigorous, very hardy, and nicely productive.

WHITE IMPERIAL is a midseason variety on a small, spreading bush. Clusters are medium to long, well filled with medium to large berries that are creamy-white, sweet, and juicy.

MINNESOTA 71 is especially good for northern areas. It is a spreading, vigorous variety that bears large, well-filled clusters of plump, good-quality berries in midseason.

WHITE GRAPE currants, the variety usually sold by nurseries, is similar to White Imperial but superior.

PERFECTION ripens in midseason. It is fairly productive with large, bright crimson berries on a somewhat spreading bush.

Some nurseries offer black currants, but they may be difficult to find.

GOOSEBERRY VARIETIES

Although European varieties of gooseberries are larger, American varieties are more productive and hardier and are considered tastier and of higher quality. Just as important, they do better in our climate and growing conditions.

DOWNING bears large, pale-green fruit. It is probably the most widely grown variety and is preferred for its canning quality, which is excellent.

GLENDALE has medium-size, dull-red fruit. This plant grows rather large and is vigorous and productive. Since it withstands heat well, it is recommended for southern areas.

FREDONIA is moderately vigorous and productive. Berries are exceptionally large, dark red, and attractive. This is probably the best English-type gooseberry available.

POORMAN belies its name. It is actually the most vigorous, healthy, and productive variety that performs well in northern areas. Its bushes are the largest of any American type, and the berries are red, attractive, and of the highest quality.

CHAUTAUQUA is medium-early and has very large fruit for dessert use. The fruit is greenish yellow; the bush is small and somewhat spreading. It may fit better into special spots where taller, more vigorous bushes would be crowded.

PLANTING POINTERS

■Currants and gooseberries need a cool, moist, and somewhat shady location. Therefore, you can grow them in spots not suited for other fruit crops. Since they are bushes, they'll fit into property borders or as groupings in corners. They will also do well interplanted with other flowering shrubs along a shady side of your house. You can use the taller-growing types along a wall. The lower-growing, spreading varieties can then be planted in front of the tall ones. This gives you a wider selection of plants plus a range of taste treats.

Currants and gooseberries are resistant to low temperatures, but with the exception of some heat-tolerant varieties, they don't thrive where summers are hot and dry. Gooseberries are generally more tolerant of heat than currants are. If you want to try these fruits in southern areas, plant them on the north side of a building that receives abundant shade. This can help protect the plants from summer's heat. Pick a site with good air circulation and well-drained soil.

Currants and gooseberries both bloom early in the spring. That means that they may be damaged by late frosts if they aren't protected. You can erect windscreens of stockade fencing or burlap fastened on poles.

Currants and gooseberries are shallow rooted. Although they require moist soil as they set their fruit, neither currants nor gooseberries can stand wet feet. They grow best in deep, fertile loam with a pH of 6.0 to 8.0. Although you can be successful with these plants in lighter soils, they prefer heavier types such as silt or clay loams. Adding abundant amounts of organic matter to a sandy soil can increase its water-holding capacity. Drainage is important, but adequate supplies of moisture are even more so.

Vigorous one-year-old plants are the best buy. Younger plants are not only less expensive but also easier for you to train and prune to desired shapes. Since pruning is also vital for successful fruit production, it is usually best to start with vigorous young plants and train them as you wish.

For a berry patch, you should plant currants and gooseberries about 4 feet apart in rows 6 to 8 feet apart. If you prefer specimens interplanted with other shrubs and bushes, allow growing room of about 4 to 6 feet in diameter, depending on the variety.

Set the plants slightly deeper in the ground than they grew in the nursery. This will cause them to grow new shoots from below the soil level. The new shoots will form bushes rather than merely single- or double-stemmed plants. Pack the soil firmly about the roots and then water well.

After planting, cut the tops of currants and gooseberries back to 8 to 10 inches. This pruning encourages side branching and bushier growth patterns.

Mulching is a sound practice for these plants. Any good organic material is fine: grass clippings, compost, peat moss, or leaf mold. Or you can try black plastic. Spread organic mulch in a 3-foot circle around each bush. Before winter, however, be certain to pull the mulch back from around the bushes. This eliminates nesting spots for mice, which are fond of feeding on young shoots.

If you don't have enough mulch material, your next best bet is clean cultivation. Weeds compete with all plants for moisture and nutrients. In order to produce abundantly, currants and similar bush fruits need nutrients, so keep weeds away from them. If you cultivate rather than mulch, just scratch the soil slightly. You don't want to disturb the shallow roots.

FEEDING

■Currants and gooseberries respond to fertilization even when growing in already fertile soil. Plan to make an annual fall or late-winter application of well-rotted barnyard or poultry manure. Spread this about 1 inch deep in a 3-foot circle around each plant, right on top of the mulch. As it rots down, it will help decompose the mulch, adding vital nutrients to the soil. These plants enjoy high organic matter in the soil—the more the better.

You can also use commercial fertilizer. If you do, apply 1 cup of 10-10-10 around each plant after planting and again each spring before the buds open. On sandier soils you should continue to build up organic matter with manure, straw, or compost each year. It also pays to increase the fertilizer rate somewhat on sandier soils, since a bit will be leached into lower levels and lost to the feeding roots. Apply 1½ to 2 cups of 10-10-10 or 10-6-4 per plant.

PRUNING

■ Gooseberries and currants form bushes with many branches rising near the original plant. Do your pruning anytime during the dormant period, when leaves are off. Pruning these bushes means thinning out excess stems. Simply snip away any rubbing branches and broken or weak stems. Shape the bushes to fit the look you want in your landscape scene. Little pruning is needed until plants are four years old.

At maturity, the typical mature bush should have three or four stems each of one-, two-, and three-year-old wood. The actual number is determined by the vigor of the bush. Since these bushes are low growing, only occasional top pruning of taller varieties is necessary to keep plants within their allotted spot.

Remove all wood over three years old, since it is less productive than young, vigorous wood. You can identify old wood by its darker, more weathered appearance. Remove any prostrate stems.

Since the best crops are borne on two- and three-year-old fruiting wood, you'll want to encourage it to continue forming from the most vigorous one-year-old branches.

Red Lake Currants

Ruby Red Stark Strawberries can become a part of your total landscape plan, adding both color and good taste.

Golden Muscat Grapes

Roxbough Blackberries

Sparkle Strawberry with developing fruit.
©Dwight Kuhn, 1987

Concord Grapes

Ruby Raspberries

Elliot Blueberries

Blackhawk Raspberries are a productive variety.

HARVESTING

■ Currants and gooseberries begin bearing the third or fourth year. They have a productive life of ten to twenty years under good culture. You can expect 5 to 15 quarts of currants per bush. Gooseberries are normally even more productive, yielding 10 to 20 quarts per bush.

Unlike other fruits, currants and gooseberries may be left on the bush for several weeks after they ripen. When you do pick the fruit, avoid bruising it. Gooseberries may sunburn or sunscald if you leave them in the sun after picking. Both fruits can be kept in the refrigerator for a time, but since they do ripen fully on the plant, it is best to use them immediately in jelly, jam, or preserves.

ELDERBERRIES
ॐ

The wild elderberry of field and fence rows has always been popular for pies and wine. Today, thanks to those ever-alert plant breeders, elderberries have been domesticated. Unfortunately, few people know or appreciate them, but they can be an unusual part of your fruit landscape.

VARIETIES

NEW YORK 21 is an offspring of Adams, an old variety. New York 21 has larger berries than most named varieties. It is somewhat small in its bushy growth but highly productive and bears earlier than many others.

NOVA was developed from Adams #2 and was introduced in 1960 by the Kentville Experiment Station in Nova Scotia. Nova produces large bushes and is one of the most productive varieties available. In trials comparing it with others in Ohio and elsewhere, Nova exceeded all other elderberry varieties in yield. It ripens quite early in the season.

YORK is more productive than Adams varieties and is larger and bushier. Early tests have substantiated that this newer variety is more productive and larger-berried than many others. It ripens later than Adams types.

If you wish to stretch the harvest season, select early, midseason, and late varieties so that blooming periods overlap for effective cross-pollination.

PLANTING AND PRUNING POINTERS

■ Elderberries are not self-fruitful, so you'll need two different varieties planted near each other to cross-pollinate and ensure a good fruit set. They like sunny locations and ample moisture. If you have a little stream nearby, that's the best spot for them. They should also have good drainage.

These bushes grow rather tall—about 4 to 6 feet—and have a spreading habit. You'll need a spot 8 to 10 feet in diameter to accommodate the two bushes required for pollinating.

Pruning is simple. Just keep bushes trimmed within their allotted space. They'll spread nicely and droop their top branches when filled with berry clusters. Since birds like elderberries, it pays to use special netting over the bushes as the berries approach maturity.

DEWBERRIES
ᗣ

Dewberries, called boysenberries in some areas, have a trailing habit and will crawl along the ground, down a slope, or even up a pole or trellis with a bit of help. The dewberry is a relative of the trailing blackberry. The youngberry, boysenberry, and loganberry are cultivated hybrids of the trailing dewberry. They trace other parts of their heritage back to crosses with blackberries and raspberries.

VARIETIES

LUCRETIA is an early berry of good quality. It is large, long, and firm but is susceptible to anthracnose and leaf spot.

BOYSENBERRY and **YOUNGBERRY** are midseason, vigorous, and moderately productive trailing types. They bear large, reddish-black berries of good quality. **FLINT, WILLIAMS,** and **THORNFREE** are semitrailing types.

PLANTING POINTERS

■ Dewberries can grow on several different types of soil, but they prefer well-drained soil with a clay or heavier loam subsoil. You should prepare the soil thoroughly and incorporate organic matter from old leaves or compost.

Pick a sunny spot if possible, although these ramblers can be planted in slightly shadier areas if they get at least 6 hours of sun a day. If you have room for them to roam, set the plants 6 feet apart in late winter or early spring. Be sure to set the bud straight up and leave old vines on so that you can locate the plants during cultivation before vines begin growing again. Don't cover the bud more than 1 inch deep.

Be careful with cultivation. These plants are shallow rooted. Just remove weeds unless you prefer to mulch, which is more desirable. Mulch retains soil moisture and provides a cushion beneath dewberries if you let them ramble on the ground.

Canes may be killed right to the ground in northern areas if they are not protected by good straw or hay mulch cover during the winter. You might also mound soil over plants after removing vines once they have finished bearing.

FEEDING

■ As soon as vines have begun growth in spring and are 1 to 2 feet long, add a quarter of a cup of 10-10-10 fertilizer around each plant. Four to six weeks later, add another half cup of fertilizer around the plants in a circle 3 feet across. If you plant rows, you can sidedress the rows with similar amounts. These plants enjoy eating well. Consequently, a postharvest feeding with another quarter of a cup of fertilizer per mature plant can keep them thriving.

TRAINING AND PRUNING

■ Dewberries need training, whether on the ground or up a fence. Simply tie the vines to a fence post or along wood or wire trellises. You can also tie individual runners together in bundles and attach them with stout cord to upright supports.

These fruit plants require little or no pruning. But when the harvest is over in the summer, cut off all the vines—new and old—and dispose of them. That step eliminates winter homes for troublesome pests, including vine borers, which bother these plants occasionally. New vines will grow next spring.

PROPAGATING

■If you discover that dewberries please your palate, it's easy to produce more. Simply cover the tips of growing plants with a handful of soil in late summer. Roots will sprout on these cane tips by spring. Snip off the old vine a foot away from the newly rooted plant, dig it up, and start more dewberries growing elsewhere.

Grapes fit into just about any landscape plan. You can grow them on a fence, along a wall, or on a trellis. Because grapes are vines, they'll climb at will. They save you ground space by allowing you to garden in the sky.

You can grow grapes in almost any part of the country, as long as you select the proper varieties for your area. As with all plants, grapes have their own particular needs. They prefer lots of sun, well-drained soil, and good air circulation. Adequate air circulation is more important with grapes than with other plants because it helps prevent certain diseases that can afflict grapes. Fortunately, plant breeders have also developed fine new varieties with built-in resistance to common problems.

VARIETIES

There are so many good varieties of white, red, blue, and green grapes for fresh eating, preserving, and wine making that it would take pages to name them all. Below I list some of the better varieties for various regions. These have been tested and found to be satisfactory—even exceptional—for home gardens. Often you can buy excellent grape varieties locally that do well in your area. Or you may wish to get catalogs from mail-order firms (see the appendices).

Plant breeders continue to develop and introduce new, improved grape varieties. Some are designed primarily for large-scale commercial growing, ease of harvest, and wine making. Others are more suited to home garden cultivation. As you shop, consider the purpose of your grapes, whether for wine making or table use (by table use I mean fresh eating as well as jelly, jam, and juice).

FOR SOUTHERN AREAS

Among blue-black types are the following:

VAN BUREN has hardy, vigorous vines for early table use.

BUFFALO has excellent quality for early table use or wine making.

FREONIA is an early to midseason variety with hardy, vigorous vines. It is a Concord-type grape.

STEUBEN is a midseason variety for table use or wine making.

CONCORD is a mid to late season grape and has a universal standard of quality for many purposes. It is the most widely grown grape in America.

MARS SEEDLESS is everything you could want in a blue grape. It has the same unbeatable flavor of Venus and Reliance on disease-resistant vines. High yielding, it usually produces the first year after planting. This patented variety ripens in mid-August in zone 6.

GLENORA SEEDLESS is a very hardy Concord type. Huge clusters of medium to large blue-black grapes ripen in mid-August in zone 6. They are extremely hardy to −10°F.

VENUS is a fat, blue-black seedless grape that combines the best of labrusca and muscat grapes for eating. It is disease-resistant and stays on the vine well, ripening in mid to late August in zone 6. (See Zone map on pages 126–127.)

For white types, try **HIMROD, INTERLAKEN,** or **SENECA**. All are early and of high dessert quality. Himrod and Interlaken are seedless; the latter is restricted to southern areas. Himrod is delicious fresh. These vines are hardy enough to thrive in the warmer areas of zone 4 and are ready to harvest in zone 6 by mid-August. Seneca is somewhat difficult to grow but is one of the best table grapes.

REMAILY grapes are the biggest, plumpest white seedless grapes you can find. They're so productive, you may have to thin the extra-large clusters. They ripen in early September in zone 6, so these can be used to stretch your grape harvest.

NIAGARA is a midseason grape with large fruit for table use or wine making.

Of red types,

DELAWARE has a high sugar content and matures in midseason, but the vines lack vigor.

CATAWBA is a late-season variety but has vigorous vines and large berries that are good for table or wine uses.

Among muscadine grapes for southern to mid-America regions, varieties worth trying are **CARLOS, MAGNOLIA, NOBLE, FRY,** and **HUNT**. As you shop for appropriate varieties of muscadine grapes, however, be aware that female vines will not have fruit if they are planted alone.

For those of you in the Deep South, there are three fine grapes:

FLAME SEEDLESS grows as far south as the Florida Keys. Sweet and juicy, these grapes are ideal for snacking and salads. They ripen in early August.

BLUE LAKE grapes love the heat. They are highly productive with the added benefit of being disease-resistant. They are marvelous fresh but equally good for juice and jelly. Ripening begins in late June in zone 9.

STOVER is a translucent light green to golden grape with a mild flavor for fresh eating or wine making. It ripens in June.

FOR NORTHERN AREAS

For climates similar to that of the Great Lakes region, white **NIAGARA** with its large, compact bunches of berries; red **DELAWARE** with its fine table and wine uses; blue **CONCORD**, that popular favorite; and red **CATAWBA** with medium-size berries are good choices.

Here's a list of grape varieties with their relative cold-hardiness. It was provided by C. A. Lunger, a horticulturist from New Hampshire, where grapes are making a comeback in home gardens and even commercially.

MOST HARDY	**HARDY**
Beta	Niagara
Blue Jay	Delaware
Red Amber	Van Buren
Clinton	Buffalo
Brighton	Foch
Concord	Agawan
Fredona	Other hybrids
Worden	
Seibel 1000	

LESS HARDY	**LEAST IN HARDINESS**
Baco 1	White Riesling
Portland	Interlaken
Steuben	Romulus
Golden Muscat	
Other hybrids	

You can, of course, decide to experiment with the more exotic varieties. Among these are Riesling, Chardonnay, Muscat, and Beaujolais. Which varieties you grow depends on your purpose. The list is long, so take your time, get advice locally on those that prove best in your area, and plant away.

CHOOSING A SITE
∾

When you consider grapes, remember that they are sturdy, stubborn, and amazingly long-lived plants. Some vineyards have been producing for decades. In Europe, there are vineyards that can trace their heritage back centuries. Grapes can withstand drought and cold. They can succeed even in quite rocky, seemingly infertile soil. Given reasonable care, grapes often outlive those who plant them and continue rewarding the generations that follow. Keep their longevity in mind as you plan permanent places for your grapevines.

The two most important considerations for grapes are good, full sun and adequate air circulation. They like well-drained soil and growing room free from frost pockets. Avoid areas where icy air settles to nip buds in spring and plants in fall. You can usually improve drainage and soil, and add fertilizer and water, but it's difficult to cut down trees or move a garage to give grapes the sun and air they must have.

Probably the best and most common use of grapes is along an existing border fence or on a special trellis. Grapes are perfect for a property border or boundary marker. They add privacy, screen undesirable views, and add eye appeal as well as taste appeal when they bear their plump clusters of fruit.

Grapes aren't fussy about the type of fence they use for support. They'll look fine along a post-and-rail or a woven-wire

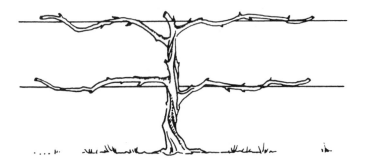

Four-arm, single-trunk Kniffin system.

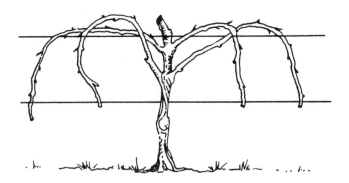

Four-arm, single-trunk umbrella system.

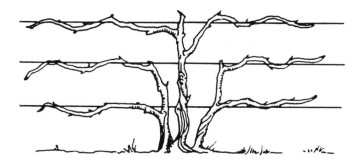

Six-arm, three-trunk, three wire modified Kniffin system.

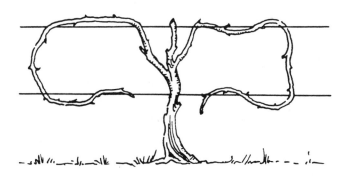

Two-arm, single-trunk umbrella system.

fence. It's best to avoid chain-link fences, since tendrils inter-twine with the wire and you can't prune properly. Avoid picket or stockade fences too, since both need periodic painting and restrict air flow around the vines.

The four-cane Kniffin system, based on an ordinary two-wire fence, is probably the favorite of grape growers and the easiest to use for home gardens. End posts should be at least 6 inches in diameter. You can use metal posts, but wood looks more natural. Select sturdy end posts 7 to 8 feet high made of cedar, redwood, or cypress, which resists rot. If you use other types, be sure that they are treated to prevent rotting in the ground. Set them 3 feet deep and case them in concrete. Posts between the anchoring end posts should be set 2 feet deep, since heavy crops can pull out shallow posts.

Space posts 8 feet apart so you can plant two grapevines be-tween each set of posts. Use #10 or #12 trellis wire that is smooth and galvanized to withstand weathering. Once the posts are set, connect the wires. The bottom wire should be 30 inches from the ground, the top one 30 inches above the first. If you want to screen an area from view, you can add another wire 30 inches above the second, making a so-called six-arm, three-wire mod-ified Kniffin system. Examine the diagrams in this chapter carefully. You can adopt a four-arm or six-arm system or choose a modified umbrella system as you prune and shape your grapevines.

The fan system is also popular for home grape growing. You can train vines to walls and fences with this hand-shaped grow-ing method. It's easy to make a trellis of poles and train the vines along each support, just as you would a climbing rose bush. Strong wires stretched in a fan shape or even a wagon-wheel shape from a T-bar support create an artistic effect. Grapes re-spond better to sculptured designing than most fruit plants.

For people who prefer a decorative approach combined with practical use, arbors are the answer. You can build arbors of all shapes and sizes, but I like those you can sit under. All you need are solid 4 x 4 timbers topped by 2 x 4 or 2 x 6 lumber. On that basic frame you can add 2 x 2s to complete a latticework, or you can use overhead and side wires instead. Vines will eventually grow up, spread out, and shade your outdoor sitting area. Design the arbor to match your home architecture. Along the sides you can plant currants or other berry bushes if you like.

PLANTING POINTERS
∾

Once established, grapevines seem to last forever. But they can try your patience in their initial slowness to get started.

Prepare your planting spot in the fall. Well-drained soil is important. If your selected area is sodded, till or spade it deep. You can improve the soil by adding compost and well-rotted manure to the existing topsoil. If the soil is heavy, be sure to add sand, peat moss, and compost to provide the drainage your vines need. Placing organic matter on the area to be planted and deep-tilling with a Rototiller pulverizes the ground well and incorporates organic material.

Test your soil's pH. If lime is needed to neutralize an acid soil, apply it before tilling.

Select vigorous one-year-old plants. Nurseries usually list these as one-year #1s. Two-year-old plants cost more, but they will give you a head start toward harvest time.

Rows should be 8 to 10 feet apart if you have room, with vines 4 to 6 feet apart in rows. For proper planting, open a hole in the ground large enough to accommodate the roots of the grapevines as they spread naturally—usually 15 to 18 inches

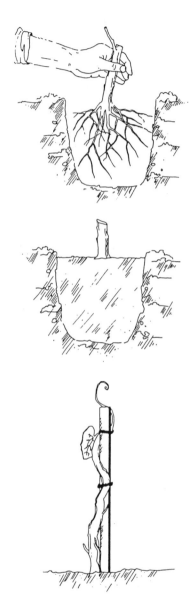

Plant your grape vine in a hole large enough to give its roots sufficient room. Fill the hole, tamp soil down, and water well. Prune as shown. As the grape vine grows, tie it to a support until it develops a strong root hold. After that, you can choose the growing and pruning system you prefer as the plant matures.

across. Plant vines the same depth as they grew in the nursery. You can usually see this point on the trunk. Keep the graft point of grafted grapes *above* the ground to discourage undesirable suckers from sprouting and taking over.

Add soil and firm it around the roots. Tamp it down. It helps to shake the plant gently to settle soil around roots. Then tamp again and add water and more soil. Finally, fill the remaining space and leave a saucer-shaped basin around the newly set plant. This lets water collect to help the vine get started right.

Water your newly planted vines regularly, especially in dry periods, until they are well started. Then be sure that they receive an inch of water each week, especially at fruiting time, to encourage the plumpest, sweetest grapes.

FEEDING
ও

Moderate amounts of fertilizer stimulate young vines to grow and maintain vigor as bearing plants. There are, of course, wide variations among soils, so one fertilizer program is not suitable for all areas. You can, however, adjust these general rules.

The first year after planting and before growth starts, apply half a cup (about a quarter of a pound) of 10-10-10 fertilizer in an 18-inch circle around each vine. Repeat this amount monthly until mid-July. You can also add compost or rotted manure as mulch to eliminate weeds and improve the soil, bit by bit, as you cultivate it into the ground at the end of each season.

The second year, double the first-year amounts. Apply 1 cup of 10-10-10 in an 18- to 24-inch circle around each vine and repeat monthly until midseason. Either cultivate around vines to remove competing weeds or mulch well.

For bearing vines, begin to apply fertilizer in early spring.

Spread 2 to 4 pounds of 10-10-10 around the plants and beneath the vines. Roots will be spreading and feeding underground over a wide area to support mature plants. Repeat with 2 pounds per vine after the fruit sets.

Grapevines have both shallow roots and deeper ones. If you cultivate rather than mulch, be sure to keep cultivation shallow to avoid damaging roots close to the surface.

Grapevines will tell you when they are well fed. Vigorous growth and plump buds indicate that they are happy. Fruiting canes of one-quarter to one-half inch in diameter—slightly larger than a pencil—and 5 to 8 feet long are desirable on most varieties. Gear your fertilizing program accordingly.

Pruning

■Knowledge of grape-growing terms is essential when it comes to pruning. The *trunk* is the main permanent stem of the plant. *Arms* are the short side extensions of the main stem. *Shoots* are the immature soft-stem growth of the current growing season. Shoots arise from buds on wood that is one or more years old and bear the leaves, flowers, and fruit. *Canes* are mature shoots; they become woody after growth has ceased. *Fruiting canes* are the one-year-old canes that are capable of and suitable for bearing fruit. *Spurs* are one-year-old canes, preferably originating near the trunk, which are pruned to just two buds. From these spur buds, shoots develop to become canes. You select one of these as a fruiting cane for the following season, thereby renewing the fruiting wood. *Suckers* are undesirable; they usually arise from the lower part of the trunk and should always be removed.

These pruning guidelines are for grapevines grown on the Kniffin system described earlier. The first year, select the best cane and shorten it to two buds. Remove all other canes along that wire. Sometimes a particular plant is especially vigorous and has one cane reaching the top wire and beyond. If so, cut the cane at the height of the top wire and tie it to the wire. Grapes may seem slow to get a roothold and start growing, but have patience. Proper pruning will reward you for many years.

The second year, select the two most vigorous canes along the top and bottom wires and tie these canes to the wires. Remove all other canes. Use strong string or coated wire to tie the canes to the wires or other supports. Wire ties can cut and damage the canes; cord or plastic-coated ties protect the tender skin and bark.

During the second growing season, select the best, strongest, and most vigorous canes for future fruit-bearing. When shoots are several inches long, remove all but three or four shoots arising from near each wire. Also remove all those on the trunk that

When a grape vine is overgrown like the one on the left, you should prune it, as shown on the right, to a six arm system to improve your vine's productivity.

are not near the wires. This may seem like heavy-handed pruning, but it's not. Surprisingly, this regimen stimulates the plants to be more prolific. After all, your goal is an abundance of grapes, not lots of foliage with little fruit.

By the third or fourth years, your grapevines should be taking their desired shape. In the dormant period preceding the third year, your plants should consist of a main trunk with several canes along each wire. Select two of the best canes at each wire and remove the others. Shorten the selected canes, leaving four to five buds on each. These buds left on the short canes will produce the shoots that will bear fruit. They will also be the source from which you'll choose next year's fruiting canes. Grapes, like other berries, bear best as these shoots become fruiting canes the second season. Therefore, you must prune each year to keep grapes prolific.

In future seasons, you should have two or more canes extending in both directions on each wire. Select a renewal spur at each of the four arms, from canes nearest the trunk. It is important to maintain fruiting wood close to the trunk and keep the entire plant within its allotted space. Grapevines will ramble far afield and be less fruitful if they are not kept in check by annual pruning.

Each year, select the fruiting canes of moderate vigor, diameter, and length that originate near the trunk and are reasonably close to the appropriate trellis wires. Remove all other growth, including sucker growth arising on the lower trunk. Shorten selected fruiting canes to six to twelve buds, depending on plant vigor. Your objective is to remove old wood so that the second-year fruiting canes can be more productive. By pruning and fertilizing properly, you'll be able to keep your vines healthy and prolific.

For the umbrella system of grape growing, begin as with the

Kniffin method. However, the objective is to select the tallest, most vigorous canes that reach the top wire. They are then allowed to flow down to the lower wire. Each year, you allow the most vigorous fruiting canes to flow so that they can be fastened to the wires, as shown in the sketch. You must, of course, let some new shoots form to become the second year's bearing wood.

Pruning for the fan system or an arbor follows the same idea. You should select the most vigorous shoots and canes, tie them to the appropriate supports, and remove all other side shoots. By removing these extra shoots and canes, you force the growing strength of the plant into the ones remaining.

DEALING WITH PESTS AND DISEASES
ᔕ

Several pests and diseases can damage your grapes. It is usually necessary to spray during the season to get fruit of consistent good quality. The grape berry moth is a common enemy; its small, greenish larvae feed on the berries. Leafhoppers—small, wedge-shaped jumping insects—feed on grape foliage. Mealybugs and flea beetles may also attack grapes. In eastern states, the Japanese beetle can be a serious problem, sometimes skeletonizing leaves. All these pests can be thwarted with a proper preventive program of pesticide application. Your county agricultural agent or garden supply dealer can tell you which pests are most common where you live and which multipurpose pesticides will protect your grapes.

Black rot is a fungus disease that attacks foliage and also fruit. Berries become blackened and shriveled. Downy and powdery mildews may also damage grapes. Mildew and fungus problems can often be prevented with proper air circulation and by not getting vine foliage wet, especially in warm weather. Soaker hoses on the ground are better than sprinklers for watering grapevines.

Birds often enjoy grapes, and they seem to favor some varieties over others. Contrary to popular belief, grapes themselves don't need sun to mature to their flavorful peak. Color and sweetness are governed by the amount of sugar produced by leaves and translocated to the fruit. Therefore, you can surround growing bunches with brown paper bags when clusters are half grown to protect them from birds. Tie the bags securely with string or twist ties. Or you can try a new type of netting, made of nylon and plastic and colored green or black. It blends with the foliage and prevents your feathered friends from eating your grape crop.

HARVESTING

Color isn't the only indicator of grape maturity. Actually, color is less reliable than other evidence. When grapes are ripe, seeds usually change from green to brown and the cluster stem turns slightly brownish and wrinkled. That's when grapes reach their peak sweetness.

Some varieties may shatter from the bunch before they are fully ripe, so keep an eye on them. Excess rain may cause split skins. Taste a few grapes periodically as they approach maturity and pick them when they please your taste buds.

PROPAGATING

To propagate new grapevines, take cuttings during the dormant season, preferably in early winter or early spring. Select sturdy canes and cut them in 10-inch lengths with three to four buds each. Slice the bottom, closest to the trunk, at a slant. Cut the top square. Tie cuttings into bundles. Place them vertically in a trench with the bottom ends several inches in the soil. Keep the soil moist and mulch with straw, leaves, or grass clippings to provide winter protection. By the time the ground is ready for planting in the spring, the cuttings should be calloused on the bottom and ready to root quickly. Place them 4 to 6 inches apart in a loamy soil that holds moisture fairly well. Insert cuttings with the top bud just above the soil surface and the other buds below the soil. In about one year, the cuttings will be ready for transplanting.

Alternatively, you can try layering your vines. Dig a shallow trench near the vine and bend one or two canes from each vine into the trench with the tips sticking up. Cover them with soil. Within a year, roots will form from underground buds. Simply sever the canes from the parent plant, and you'll have new stock to plant.

As you develop your skills, you may branch out into grafting new and better varieties on more common rootstock.

Home-grown raspberries are among the sweetest treats a garden can yield. You have a choice of red, purple, black, or amber-colored fruit, each distinctively different and delicious.

Raspberries thrive in almost any type of soil except the lightest sand and heaviest clays, and even those soils can be improved by following the steps in Chapter 2. That means that raspberries can be planted in areas that are less desirable for other trees or crops. Raspberries do best in horticultural zone 4—from the middle south of the United States to Canada.

8

RASPBERRIES

You have a choice of shapes and forms too. Black and purple types have a distinctive spreading and drooping habit. They can be used in small groups to provide a mound effect in the landscape. Even a few plants will provide several quarts of good eating every year. Red raspberries, normally larger and more succulent, are better used along a property line or as hedges. These varieties tend to grow upright in thickets. You can train them somewhat, but they'll do just as well with little care in an unused part of your land. If you have room, try several double rows along a walk or path. Another good use is to produce a screen effect.

Raspberries are somewhat like blackberries. The red varieties have a fondness for wandering by sucker growth arising from their roots. Black and purple types propagate themselves as their canes touch the ground and set new plants from growing tips. It's easy to keep them in bounds, but you must pay attention to pruning once or twice a year.

VARIETIES
∾

Research by Dr. R. H. Converse of the U. S. Department of Agriculture at the Research Station in Beltsville, Maryland, has revealed that raspberry plants may be infected with viruses. Although these plant diseases may not produce symptoms, they can reduce plant vigor and yield. When you buy your foundation stock, get a guarantee from the nursery that the plants are from virus-free parent plants and are disease-free themselves. This precaution saves future worries and ensures hardier, more abundant plants that will yield rewardingly.

RED RASPBERRIES

HERITAGE is a vigorous grower and is everbearing. It produces many suckers to fill in rows quickly. Plants are winter-hardy and produce moderate summer crops plus a bonus—a fall crop of medium-size, firm, excellent-quality berries. In areas as far north as New York State, berries may yield into September until the first hard frost. Canes are sturdy and erect and seldom require support.

HILTON is the largest of all red raspberries. It maintains its size throughout the season. Berries are long, conical, medium red, firm, and of good quality. It ripens in late midseason and is vigorous and self-supporting.

NEWBURG has been around for some time. It produces firm berries with fine quality and good flavor.

TAYLOR is another excellent variety for home use. Plants are tall, vigorous, hardy, and productive. Berries are large, conical, firm, red, and tasty.

CITADEL is a midseason producer of large berries and grows vigorously.

COMET is a promising hardy variety, somewhat resistant to anthracnose and spur light.

MILTON is a late variety, more tolerant to mosaic than most. It produces tall canes but is not as hardy in colder areas as others.

MADAWASKA RED has a tough cane and is hardy in the northern United States and into Canada. Berries are huge and ripen in midseason.

NEW HAMPSHIRE is another midseason ripener with large, well-flavored fruit.

BOYNE is a new red variety from Canada. It stands up well to cold and has hardy, strong canes and flavorful fruit.

AUGUST RED is an everbearing type for northern areas. It begins to produce in late July and continues to bear plump, delicious red berries for weeks.

RUBY RED is a Watson cultivar, the first raspberry combining fall bearing and jumbo size. Favored by commercial growers for its spring and heavy fall crops, it is gaining popularity everywhere.

DORMANRED is a plump, bright-red berry that enjoys southern climates. You'll pick big crops every summer beginning in mid-June in zone 9.

SOUTHLAND does well in the mid-South. Plants are vigorous, disease-resistant, and highly productive.

TITAN JUMBO berries live up to their name, and the canes bear twice the crop of most others. Better yet, this one is almost thornless. A patented red raspberry, it ripens in early June in zone 6. (*See Plant Hardiness Zone chart on pages 126–127.*)

BLACK RASPBERRIES

ALLEN is a newly named variety that is vigorous and productive. It bears large, attractive fruit, a large portion of which is pickable at one time.

BRISTOL is well known in northern areas for its large, firm, glossy, high-quality berries. Plants are hardy, vigorous, and productive.

DUNDEE is a popular variety for commercial growing. It also does well in home gardens, producing vigorous plants even in imperfectly drained soils. It is similar to Bristol.

HURON has large, glossy, attractive berries on vigorous, hardy plants. It is not too susceptible to anthracnose.

JEWEL is a relatively new variety dating from 1973. It is not susceptible to any serious diseases and is only slightly affected by mildew. Fruits are large, glossy, and high-quality. Plants are vigorous, hardy, and nicely productive.

LOGAN or **NEW LOGAN** is early to ripen and yields heavily.

BLACK HAWK is a very late but productive variety. The fruit is good for fresh use, freezing, jams, or jellies.

PURPLE RASPBERRIES

CLYDE is a midseason to late-ripening variety, moderately hardy, and consistently productive. Berries are darker than medium purple, firm, and tart.

NEW YORK 905 is a promising new purple raspberry in its introductory stages. It is not a true purple but resembles this type more than red or black. It has large, round, firm reddish-purple berries. Stocks are scarce at present, but the Geneva Fruit Testing Association has them, and they're worth trying.

SODUS is another purple variety. It is very productive on hardy, drought-resistant bushes and is good for dessert, freezing, or cooking. It is somewhat susceptible to mosaic and verticillium problems.

LIGHT-COLORED RASPBERRIES

AMBER is a very vigorous variety with large, amber-colored, sweet-tasting berries.

SEPTEMBER is also light but is more red in color. It bears one crop early and another in early fall, except in northern areas, where early frosts may hit the plants and damage berries before the major fall crop is ready.

PLANTING POINTERS
ᐁ

Although raspberries can grow reasonably well on less than the best soils, they'll reward you more abundantly if you pick the most desirable site for them. A well-drained soil with liberal amounts of humus added year by year will increase their productivity. Sandier soils, including sandy loams, tend to dry. Unless you provide ample moisture at fruiting time, raspberries just won't be as juicy and sweet.

Good sun is important with red varieties. The black ones can do quite well with partial shade, provided they get a fair share of sunlight for several hours each day.

A site on ground higher than surrounding areas is desirable for raspberries. Cool spring air drains away from such areas, avoiding nipped buds and reduced crops. In comparing level sites with gentle slopes, many gardeners believe that a slope somehow improves success with raspberry bushes.

Before you plant in spring, prepare the soil well. It pays to pick a site where cultivated crops were grown the year or years before, because the soil is usually in better condition. If you must choose a site in sod, dig or till the sod under the fall before planting, but first spread lime and 10-6-4 or similar fertilizer on the area. When you turn the sod under, this fertilizer helps decompose the organic matter, including old plant roots. With raspberries, as with most other berry crops, the more you can improve the aeration and structure of the soil with increased amounts of organic matter, the better the plant growth will be.

If you prepare the berry site in early fall, plant a cover crop of rye grass. Its roots will penetrate deep and open the soil. Then till this green manure under come spring planting time. If animal manure is available, plow it under too to incorporate even more organic material into the soil. You can mulch around established raspberry plantings, but clean cultivation several times a season seems to produce more favorable results. Therefore, it pays to incorporate as much organic matter as possible into the chosen area before planting. As with blackberries, it also pays to destroy any wild raspberries in the area. They may tolerate and harbor diseases, acting as carriers to infect your domesticated varieties.

Raspberries are self-fruitful, but selecting several varieties offers different tastes and improved cross-pollination. It also provides the pleasure of early-, mid-, and late-season harvests. One-year-old rooted stock is the best buy. These are young suckers from the current season's growth. Unlike grape suckers, raspberry suckers are good things. They are new canes that sprout to produce the next year's fruiting wood.

Raspberries are susceptible to crown gall disease, anthracnose, and some other wilt diseases, so be sure that the plants you buy are from a reliable nursery and certified virus-free. Discard any canes that have wartlike growths or galls on roots or crown areas.

In rows, plant your raspberries 3 to 4 feet apart. Space rows 6

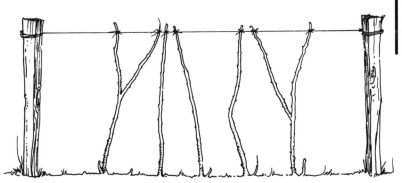

Training and pruning red raspberries—hedge row system.

to 8 feet apart for red varieties. Black and purple raspberries also respond to hill cultivation. This means simply planting them in such a way that a bushy mound results. If you elect to use the hill system, plant young rootstock 5 feet apart each way, allowing a 5-foot diameter for each plant to mature. You can also plant red, black, and purple varieties closer together to encourage faster fill-in of the rows or the corner in which they are to become established. Reds can be planted a foot apart and in hills 3 feet apart. Attention to pruning will keep them in bounds.

Since raspberries are softer-caned than blackberries, it helps to keep roots moist and to shape a ball of soil around the small roots when planting. You can spread the roots too, but always keep them moist. Fill the soil around the new plants, tamp it firmly to settle it, and water well. When transplanting suckers from an established area to a new one, dig and plant the suckers immediately. You may lose a large proportion if they dry out.

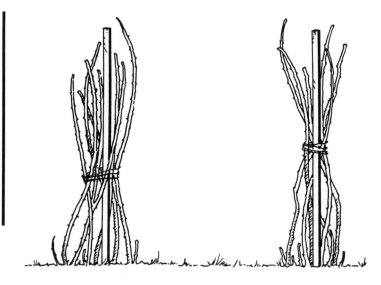

Training and pruning red raspberries—hill system.

After planting, prune canes back to half their size. Keep watering them every few days until new buds sprout on the canes. After that, watering once a week is sufficient as they establish a sturdy roothold. Mulching in an 18- to 24-inch circle around new plants the first year is advisable. However, raspberries respond best to clean cultivation after they are well-rooted and growing vigorously.

All raspberries are shallow rooted. When you cultivate, be certain to do it lightly. Just remove weeds by scratching the soil to avoid damaging the feeding roots barely beneath the surface. Sometimes hand weeding is best. If you cultivate too deeply, you may cut roots, thereby encouraging many new suckers to grow. Soon you will have a tangle rather than the tidy and productive plants you want. This characteristic is more common with red varieties than others.

FEEDING

〜

Although they can produce on poor soils, raspberries are another fruit that responds well to tender loving care, which includes providing manure or commercial fertilizer to nourish them. It also includes adding compost as a mulch and lightly raking it into the soil each fall to improve soil texture and structure as well as to provide minute amounts of nutrients.

If you can get manure, spread it about 2 inches deep along the rows each spring. You might introduce some weed seeds along with barnyard manure, so be alert for weeds. Pull them out gently when they sprout.

Raspberries can use a moderate amount of fertilizer the first year. For every bush, spread a quarter of a cup of 10-10-10, or less of 16-16-16, in a circle around each plant. You can also apply this as a band on each side of the row.

The second year, when new suckers have sprouted and your raspberries are setting their permanent pattern, apply 3 to 5 pounds of complete 10-10-10 along each 100 feet of row. Split the amount so that each side gets half the total. On black and purple raspberries grown in hills or as bushes, a cup or two of this fertilizer around the bush is sufficient in spring.

Avoid fertilizing in summer. It increases tender cane growth and contributes to winterkill. Late fertilizing may also encourage excess sucker growth, which means more pruning work for you.

The first two years, your raspberries may seem to be off to a surprisingly slow start. Take heart; that's just their way. Use that space between rows or around bushes for other plants during this period. If you don't want to grow other crops, plant a green manure crop of rye, oats, or clover and dig it under in the spring. That way, you'll be improving nearby soil areas so that as your

RASPBERRIES

raspberry plants spread, they'll find excellent soil conditions to welcome their expanding root systems.

If you mulch your raspberries with sawdust and wood chips or similar materials, remember that these cellulose mulches need extra nitrogen to decompose properly. Spread a cup of nitrogen fertilizer on top of the mulch around each plant or along every few feet of row. It will do wonders for the plants as it helps the woodier mulches perform their function.

Raspberries need lots to drink when they bloom and begin to set their fruits. If you receive less than an inch of water each week, be sure to supplement it. To measure the water you apply, set straight-sided cans or cups in the rows. When an inch of water is collected in them, that's enough for the week.

If a drought hits hard, a second watering each week may be needed to replace the moisture lost down into the subsoil. Raspberries feed with shallow roots, so the top layer of soil needs the water. Soaker hoses are best. Avoid sprinkling late in the day, since excess moisture on foliage and fruit can cause mildews and molds. If these problems occur, a late fungicide application may help, but preventing the problem is wiser.

PRUNING
ॐ

RED RASPBERRIES

■ The first year, cut red raspberries to within 6 to 8 inches of the ground. Your plants will become rooted faster if you pick off any blossoms that occur the first year. The second year, a partial crop will form. From the third year on, you'll be rewarded by buckets of berries.

During the second year, remove any broken and damaged canes. If some have grown too tall, you may top them back to a

manageable height. This encourages the desired side growth of
lateral branches. Prune back to an outside bud to ensure bushier
growth.

The third spring is generally the critical pruning time. The
pruning you do now is what you have to do each year to keep
bushes productive, vigorous, and untangled. Cut off about one-
quarter of the length of the canes that grew the previous season.
This should leave canes 24 to 36 inches high, except for taller-
growing varieties, whose top height should be 48 inches.
Although pruning encourages necessary side branching, over-
pruning reduces yields. Raspberries must be trimmed, but not as
much as other fruits need to be.

Remove weak, thin, and dead canes. All canes that show any
evidence of disease should be removed and burned at a distance
from the raspberry bushes. Pruning time is also a good opportu-
nity to look for cankers, galls, or other problems. If you find any,
check other canes nearby. Remove any afflicted canes and destroy them; never use them for compost. This holds true for diseased leaves of any plant, since some diseases can live even in
the heat of active compost piles.

Raspberries are biennial. New canes appear, mature, and become next year's fruiting wood. After that they die and should
be removed. Fruit is borne on second-year wood, so allow that
and new young canes to continue growing. Thin these young
canes only enough to keep plants reasonably open to sun and air
and to prevent overcrowding.

BLACK AND PURPLE RASPBERRIES

■ Black and purple raspberries should be pruned differently,
since their growth habit is different from red varieties. As you
inspect your black and purple raspberries during the spring, re-

On the left is an overgrown black raspberry plant. On the right is the way it should look after proper pruning.

move dead, diseased, or weak canes as you would with red varieties. Thicker canes are more productive, so eliminate those less than a quarter of an inch in diameter at the base, where the cane rises from the soil.

The blacks and purples should be topped in summer during the first season to promote side branching. Topped plants also make harvesting easier and reduce wind damage. Canes may sprout rapidly on good soil, so more than one summer pruning may be needed.

Remove the top 3 to 4 inches of growth when the cane has reached a height of 24 to 36 inches. If plants are less vigorous, cut canes at 18 to 24 inches. Don't prune in late summer, or you will encourage new side shoots that are easily damaged by winter weather.

After topping back, prune laterals of the main canes 8 to 12 inches in length on black varieties, 18 to 24 inches on purple ones. Purple varieties produce more fruitful buds farther from the main cane, so you should leave them slightly longer. The larger the cane, the more fruiting wood that can be left.

If you are using the hill system for black and purple raspberries, simply remove suckers that arise in other than the desired area. Digging is best, since breaking or pruning may leave the small roots intact to sprout again.

A Rototiller does a good job eliminating suckers that tend to fill in between rows and make harvesting difficult. It also enables you to spread fertilizer and manure and do your pruning more easily than if the plants were allowed to form a matted thicket.

DEALING WITH PESTS
ᴖᴗ

Insects can be a problem, but they are readily controlled by well-timed pesticide applications. It is important to keep insects away, because they can transmit plant diseases. With raspberries especially, plant diseases are more of a threat than insects alone. It is best to consult local pesticide suppliers or county agents for the latest pest-control programs suggested in your state.

One interesting fact is worth noting. Insects prefer to attack weak, less-than-healthy plants. This is true for both vegetables and fruits. The better you care for your plants, the better they can resist insects and diseases.

HARVESTING
ᴖᴗ

After several years, a well-established red raspberry planting should yield 50 to 100 pints of tasty berries per 100 feet of row. Black and purple raspberries yield somewhat less.

Picking time is important. Although red raspberries may last for a while on the bush, it is generally best to pick them as soon as they are ripe. Otherwise, fruit will deteriorate in just a few days, and you can lose a large portion of your crop. That's especially true with black and purple types.

At their peak, berries may have to be harvested several times a week, especially if the weather remains hot. Here's how to tell when they're ready: Raspberries are perfect for picking when they separate easily from the "core," without crumbling or mushing. Grasp a sample berry firmly between thumb and two fingers. Pull with an even pressure. If it pops off handily, tastes juicy and sweet, and is not oversoft, you're right on time.

Harvest in the coolness of morning. It is important to use pint or quart containers. If you pile berries in a deep container, the weight of the top berries will crush those below. Excess handling also causes bruising and loss of quality.

Move raspberries from picking basket to refrigerator quickly. Berries will keep for several days under refrigeration, but if you plan to can them or make jam, jelly, or preserves, do it as soon as possible.

Berries can also be frozen. After washing them to remove soil, grit, and dust, dry them on absorbent paper towels. Then place them on a cookie sheet in the freezer. They'll quickly freeze, making it easy to pack them into containers for storage.

PROPAGATING
෮

Raspberries are easy to reproduce. Red varieties do it themselves. New suckers sprout all around the plants and along the rows. Usually each parent plant produces five or six new plants a year. Just dig up the extras that you don't need for next year's

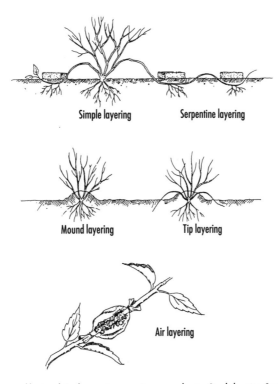

Simple layering · Serpentine layering · Mound layering · Tip layering · Air layering

There are several basic and simple ways to propagate your raspberries: Simple layering, Serpentine layering, Mound layering, Tip layering, and Air layering.

fruiting wood and replant them elsewhere. Avoid using any that are weak or thin or that show any signs of disease. Transplant any suckers immediately after digging. The best time to transplant is spring, but early fall is satisfactory if you mulch them the first year.

Black and purple types are propagated differently—by tip layering. In fall, when the tips of the current year's lateral canes appear "rat-tailed" or with small curled leaves at the tip, just tuck these tips into the soil at a distance from the parent plant. Cover each one well with a shovelful of soil. You can bend laterals so they touch the ground if they aren't quite ready and tuck the tips in. Use a small stone or wire hook to hold a cane if it's springy and tends to snap out of the soil.

By late fall, the laterals are usually well rooted, but it is best to leave the new plants until spring. Cover them with a mulch to mark them. In spring, sever the new plants from the parent, leaving an 8- to 10-inch portion as a handle to make moving and transplanting easier. Dig the newly rooted plants and set them wherever you want to establish more raspberries. Then prune as you would with one-year-old stock from a nursery and follow the recommended procedure year by year until your new areas are bearing abundantly.

Strawberries are the most popular home garden fruit grown in America. You can grow them from Florida to Alaska. They require little room or care and produce an abundant fruit supply.

You can grow them in rows, in hills, in window boxes, in patio planters, along a path, or interplanted with flowers and vegetables. They can even be used as a ground cover near your shrubs.

With proper care, just twenty-five plants in less than 50 feet of row will yield 25 to 40 quarts of berries. New everbearing varieties yield extra abundantly. By selecting several different varieties, you can enjoy strawberries from spring through late fall.

9

STRAWBERRIES

Strawberry plants have a way of replenishing themselves. Runners from mature plants create new plants that will eventually produce fruit. Once you set a bed or two, you'll have strawberries for many years to come.

VARIETIES

Listed below are some of the best strawberry varieties, developed by plant breeders to produce the highest yields of the most flavorful, hardy, and season-stretching berries. Old-time disease problems have been virtually eliminated by the availability of virus-free plants and improved disease-resistant varieties.

Your choice among strawberries is wide. Since 1920, more than one million different seedling varieties have been evaluated by U.S. Department of Agriculture researchers and experiment-station workers in various states. The best have been introduced to fit the needs of various growing regions. It pays to compare test plantings of new offerings from time to time, since improved varieties can outyield even old favorites.

SUNRISE is an early, large, tart, and bright-colored fruit.

RARITAN is an early midseason berry of excellent quality. It is very productive with high-quality, attractive fruit.

SURECROP is another midseason variety with large, light-red, firm, tart berries. It is good for freezing.

SPARKLE is a midseason variety that is very productive, with medium-firm, high-quality berries. It is vigorous in producing runners for new plants.

CATSKILL is a midseason variety. It is very productive and has large berries that tend to be soft. They are best used fresh.

JERSEYBELL is late, productive, large, and of good quality.

FLETCHER is vigorous and produces many runners. Flowers are somewhat resistant to frost. Berries are medium, firm, glossy, and of good quality. This is a fine variety for fresh use or freezing, slightly better than Sparkle.

GALA is very early with large, slightly dark, rough berries. Plants are vigorous and productive and fruit well without crowding. Avoid planting Gala in frosty areas, since it blooms exceptionally early.

GARNET is a promising new variety. Berries are large, medium red, moderately firm, and of good quality.

HOLIDAY is a new, firm-fruited variety. Plants are productive and vigorous and make well-matted rows; berries are large, bright red, glossy, and aromatic. They ripen in midseason and are fine for fresh use, freezing, or preserving.

CARDINAL is sweeter than most strawberries and grows in most types of soil. Its flavor, high yields, and disease-resistance will make it a big favorite.

StarkRuby Red is a patented Aliso cultivar from Stark. This exceptionally large berry is very vigorous.

Stark Crimson King is a trademarked and patented variety, a Hagking cultivar. Some grow up to 5 inches around and are consistent winners at fairs and contests. They are firm, disease-resistant, and hardy.

Among the newer everbearing strawberries, **Geneva** is a fine one. **Ozark Beauty** is delightfully sweet. **Gem, Superfection**, and **Streamliner** are others that do well.

Because nurseries are continually introducing new and improved types, check their recommendations. When you shop, either locally or by mail, depend on well-established, reliable plant nurseries. The appendices include a list of reputable firms.

Choosing a Site and a Planting Method

Although strawberries are available that will thrive in any climate and have a fair tolerance for various types of soil, they perform best when the site is right and the soil is to their liking. Pick an area with lots of sun. Avoid frost pockets to prevent nipping of the buds when they bloom in early spring. A gentle slope is perfect; so is an area protected from harsh winds. Strawberries prefer soils with high organic matter. If your soil lacks it, you can easily till under compost, peat moss, manure, or similar materials to enrich the existing soil.

Avoid using ground that has been planted with tomatoes, peppers, eggplants, or raspberries within the last two years. Some diseases that afflict these plants may remain in the soil to slow or stunt strawberry plants. Be sure that your soil has good drainage. Strawberry roots are shallow, and when air pores in the soil are constantly clogged with water, the roots can't pull up the needed nutrients to reach out to feed as well.

When possible, plant a green manure crop of rye the previous year. Whether you do this or not, plan to apply 2 pounds of a high-phosphorus and high-potash fertilizer such as 6-24-24 per 100 square feet before turning the soil. Nitrogen is needed to build vegetative growth for trees and bushes, but strawberries rely on phosphorus and potash to attain their best fruit set and sweetest taste.

ROWS OR HILLS

■You can select among three types of strawberry beds:

1. The matted row, in which plants mass together.

2. The spaced row, in which you remove some plants to give those remaining more room to spread individually.

3. The hill system, in which individual plants are given ample room to perform to perfection by themselves.

Most commercial growers prefer the matted row method, since it produces greater yields per acre. That's not so critical in home plantings, since you can get fine results with the other methods. For matted rows, space plants 2 feet apart. If you have the room, plant several rows 4 to 5 feet apart.

Runners (so-called daughter plants) are sent out by the parents to root in all directions. Your rows will eventually become densely populated by new plants. Cultivation is somewhat difficult with these tangled, matted rows, but the plants require little

Row system

weeding or other care. Final width of the row should be about 2 to 2½ feet. Plants will be about 8 inches apart when the row is fully filled in. The advantages of the matted row system are high yields and ease of care. Disadvantages are crowding of plants, slightly smaller berries, and susceptibility to disease and drought.

The spaced row system begins the same as a matted row. Space plants 2 feet apart with rows 4 to 5 feet apart. The object is to have a bed 15 to 18 inches wide, with new plants from runners spaced 7 to 10 inches apart. You remove the excess plants that are too close together so that the nutrients, moisture, and sunlight are concentrated on fewer plants, encouraging stronger

Hill System

growth and bigger berries. You can modify this spaced row system even further by removing more plants.

With the hill system, you remove all runners as they form. That way, the original plants are the only ones that produce berries. The distance between rows can be narrow, since rows are really only one plant wide. Spacing within rows should be close, about one plant every foot. You can plant several parallel rows. The individual plants will develop large and numerous crowns and bear more fruit than individual plants in other systems.

The advantages of the hill method are larger and more berries per plant and easier weeding and picking. However, you'll need more plants to start your strawberry patch. Also, it takes extra effort to remove those constantly sprouting runners every few weeks during the spring and summer. Another point is worth considering: If you don't let plants set new runners, you'll have no new plants to start new areas or replenish the bed as older plants become less productive.

Strawberry plants are most prolific their second and third years. After that, the original plants become tired and don't bear as well. It's important to let runners multiply to some extent so that your beds replenish themselves. For this reason, a modified matted row seems best for home garden purposes.

A STRAWBERRY PYRAMID

■A handy way to grow strawberries even when ground space is limited is to build a three-level strawberry pyramid. All you need is an area 6 feet by 6 feet. Using 2 x 6-inch planks, make the bottom level 6 feet square, the middle level 4 feet square, and the top level 2 feet square. Redwood or cedar boards are best, since they resist decay.

Prepare your soil mixture using 13 bushels of topsoil, 5

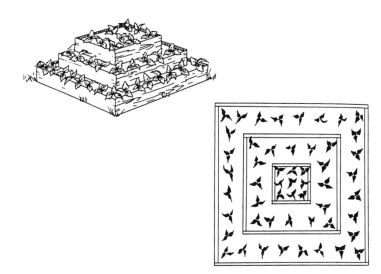

If your space is limited, try a pyramid strawberry bed.

bushels (or the typical 6-cubic-foot bale) of peat moss, and 5
bushels of perlite or sand. Mix one pound of 5-10-10 or 6-12-12
fertilizer with the soil. You can blend the material with a shovel,
mixing alternate layers until the consistency is even.

Lay the largest frame on a level surface in a sunny location
and fill it with soil, firming the mixture to avoid later settling.
Next, position and fill the middle frame, and then the top frame.
Tamp the soil down firmly. You can anchor the frame with stakes
in the ground if you wish. Keep the soil weed-free until you're
ready to plant.

Setting the strawberry plants 9 inches apart will give you
twenty-eight on the first level, sixteen on the second, and nine
on the top, for a total of fifty-three plants in one 6-foot-square
space. The top level can be somewhat more closely spaced. Plan
to water the pyramid each week, especially when plants are set-

ting fruit. You can mulch all three levels with peat moss to help retain soil moisture.

Some gardeners set a dwarf fruit tree in the top of the pyramid, digging down far enough for its roots to be well spread. If you do this, you'll have to pay closer attention to feeding and watering each year to supply the necessary nutrients for both the tree and your strawberries. However, such an arrangement provides an interesting and multipurpose planter where space is tight.

A STRAWBERRY BARREL

■ If you have even less space—maybe only a balcony or a porch—you still can enjoy luscious ripe strawberries in season: Try a strawberry barrel. Hardware stores and garden centers sell these wooden barrels or variations made from ceramic material. You can also make your own from an old nail keg or storage barrel found at a flea market or garage sale. Never, however, use a barrel that has contained chemicals or other materials harmful to plants.

The first step is to drill holes around the barrel as shown in the illustration. They should be about 1½ inches in diameter and 6 to 8 inches apart, depending on the size of the barrel. You can then paint or whitewash the barrel to match the color of your house or patio furniture.

When the barrel is dry, set it on the ground or raised on four bricks. Fill the bottom with 2 to 4 inches of coarse gravel, small stones, or broken flower-pot parts. This layer provides good drainage. Excess water can escape rather than clog the soil and rot roots. Buy a piece of perforated pipe from a plumbing supply store, or make your own from stovepipe by punching holes in it. Place this pipe in the center of the barrel supported by the gravel in the base.

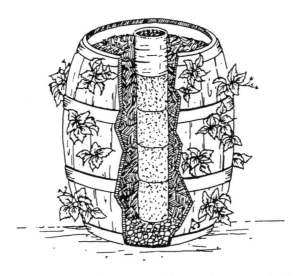

For a porch, balcony, or city roof top, you can grow delicious strawberries in a strawberry barrel.

The next step is to fill the bottom of the barrel with the same soil mixture as described for the strawberry pyramid. You can use leaf mold, peat, or compost and combine these organic materials with good topsoil. If you live in an apartment and have no access to good garden soil, garden centers often sell small bags of peat moss and dried compost as well as 25-pound bags of potting soil. Fill the barrel to the level of the lowest circle of holes. Spread the roots of the plants horizontally and evenly and add more soil. Be sure that the crowns of the plants are just at the opening in the barrel. Continue filling the barrel with soil and planting until you reach the top, then pour gravel into the pipe. That gravel core provides a fine watering system and also lets excess water drain back from the soil after a rain or in case you overwater.

You can plant twelve to twenty-four strawberries in a small to medium barrel. Larger barrels will accommodate even more.

Care is similar to that for ground-planted strawberries. A little balanced fertilizer, strong on the phosphorus and potash sides, can be mixed with water to feed your barrel plants during the season as they begin to set their fruits.

Strawberries also make a lovely hanging basket. Just a few plants in good soil will reward you with a pint or more of berries. Window boxes and patio planters are other potential spots for strawberries.

PLANTING POINTERS
ᖡ

Strawberries should be planted as early in the spring as possible—as soon as the soil is warm and crumbly. Nurseries normally ship bare-root plants wrapped in moist sphagnum moss. Garden centers sell plants in polybags or composition paper pots. If the ones you buy are bare-rooted, put them in a pail of water containing one cup of compost. Plant the strawberries as soon as you can, and don't let the roots dry out. Strawberry planting requires strict attention to the level of the crowns to ensure success—not too high, not too low, but with the crown just at the soil surface.

Although your mouth may be watering for strawberries the first year, resist the urge to let them bloom and set fruit, except for everbearing varieties, which will bear a crop in the fall. All spring and summer bearing varieties, however, need the first year to become established. It pays in terms of future abundant harvests to pinch off any flowers that appear the first year. This also encourages ample runner formation, which is your primary objective the first year, unless you prefer the hill system of individual plants. Those new plants formed from runners will produce the major share of your crop next year.

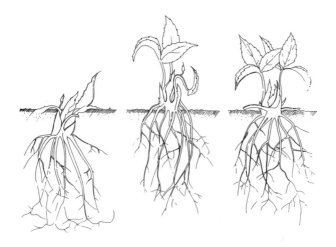

When you plant strawberries, consult this illustration. The first shows a strawberry plant planted too deeply, the second, one planted too high. The third illustrates the proper position for planting your strawberries.

FEEDING AND WEEDING
∾

If plant growth seems slow in mid-June, apply 1 pound of a complete-analysis 10-10-10 or 12-12-12 fertilizer per 50 feet of row. Spread half a pound along each side of the row. Scratching lightly and watering after application lets the plant food dissolve and go to work to boost strawberry growth. Keep fertilizer particles off the leaves to prevent chemical burns.

You must weed your strawberry bed, since weeds steal nutrients and moisture. Pull larger weeds and mulch as much as possible with organic materials to smother smaller weeds. Another possibility is to place black plastic in position before you plant; you then slit holes in the plastic and plant the strawberries through the slits. Organic mulch is better, however. It conserves moisture, smothers weeds, looks nicer, and adds nutrients to the soil and improves its texture.

HARVESTING
∾

Strawberries begin bearing in June and can last late into summer. As berries become red, plump, and ripe, pick a few. Your taste and the berries' appearance are the best indicators of harvest time. Several pickings will be necessary.

If you have any surplus berries, you can save them. Strawberries are easy to freeze, which is the best way to save them for use throughout the off-season. Wash them first, then pack them fresh in quart or pint containers. Or you might want to prepare syrup or jam.

WINTERING OVER
∾

In areas with severe winters, you may need to protect your strawberry plants from frost heaving, which can uproot and kill them. Old bales of hay or straw work well, as do piles of dried leaves. However, don't use diseased leaves, especially from fruit trees. Each spring as the weather warms, remove the cover mulch in two phases: about half as snow is gone, the rest from the tops of plants when it really warms up. Leave mulch around the plants to smother weeds.

REPLENISHING THE BED
∾

By the second year, you'll be enjoying more fruit than you thought possible from so few plants. The third year should also produce a heavy crop. After that, you may notice a decline in yield. At that time, you have some options:

1. You can remove the older plants and let the younger ones that sprout from runners become the parent plants. This simple renovation takes a few hours but is well worthwhile.

2. You can transplant the new plants and start another bed.

3. You can rotate several areas every few years.

The third option works as follows: First you start a bed. The second year, as you remove excess runners to prevent an overly matted row, begin another bed. After the third year, when the initial bed begins decreasing in productivity, the next bed is increasing. The fourth year, completely remove the original bed and renovate the soil by adding organic matter. Then replant it with excess runner plants from the second bed. In this way, you rotate your renovation to keep your plants as prolific as possible.

Whether you like it or not, insect enemies and plant diseases can attack even the best-tended fruit trees and bushes. Although it's true that healthy, vigorous plants have some ability to withstand and fight off disease and insect problems, conditions sometimes favor the pest and not your plants. Before that time comes, it helps to know some of the arch villains that may visit your home fruit planting. They're not particularly nice to know, but if you can spot these problems and pests before they launch full-scale attacks, they are easier to defeat.

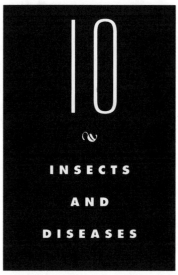

Prevention of problems before they occur has its obvious advantages. Chemical sprays can prevent most insect and disease problems. There are safe materials that can stop pests yet have few, if any, adverse effects on people or the environment.

Here's a list of the most troublesome insects for bush and tree fruits. Insect guides and literature from pesticide manufacturers provide close-up details about these insect enemies so that you can identify them and learn how to eliminate them.

COMMON INSECTS

BLACKBERRY	*aphid, cutworm, Japanese beetle, cane borer*
BLUEBERRY	*blueberry maggot, Japanese beetle*

CURRANT AND GOOSEBERRY	*currant aphid, currant worm, gooseberry caterpillar*
GRAPE	*leafhopper, Japanese beetle, rose chafer, white grub, red spider, grasshopper*
STRAWBERRY	*cane borer, cutworm, crown borer, sawfly, strawberry weevil, curculio, spittlebug*

APHIDS (PLANT LICE) attack the foliage of many types of fruit. These small, soft-bodied insects suck juice from leaves, causing them to crackle or curl. Aphids are usually green, brown, or black.

CURRANT FRUITFLIES lay eggs under the skin of currant and gooseberry fruits. Larvae feed on fruit seeds and pulp, which turns red and drops to the ground.

CYCLAMEN MITES are tiny pests. They live in the crowns of strawberry plants and attack leaves and flower buds. Leaves become wrinkled and brown at the tips. Mites may prevent fruit formation or cause misshapen fruit.

LEAFHOPPERS are green, gray, or tan, about an eighth of an inch long. They feed on the undersides of the leaves of many fruits. Young hoppers suck juice from leaves. They may transmit diseases from one tree to another.

RASPBERRY FRUITWORMS feed on young buds, leaves, and blossoms. Adults are small, light-brown beetles about an eighth of an inch long. Yellowish-white larvae live in or on ripening fruit.

RASPBERRY SAWFLIES are black, thick-bodied insects about a quarter of an inch long. They lay eggs on raspberry plants when the leaves begin to unfold. Small, spiny, green larvae feed on the leaves.

SCALE INSECTS are small sucking insects about a tenth of an inch long. Except for a brief period when the young are hatched, scale insects remain attached to a branch or twig. Oystershell scale is brownish and has a shape similar to that of an oyster shell. Scurfy scale is white and pear-shaped.

SPIDER MITES are tiny insectlike pests that suck juices from leaves, which eventually become bronzed and dried and fall. Spider mites are troublesome during dry years. Their presence may be detected by fine webs on the undersides of leaves. Wetting trees with a garden hose often aids in control.

STRAWBERRY WEEVILS are small, reddish-brown snout beetles up to an eighth of an inch long. They feed on the stems of fruit buds, which wilt or drop off.

TARNISHED PLANT BUGS are brownish bugs about a quarter of an inch long. They feed on strawberries and other plants, damaging foliage and fruit. Both adults and nymphs injure plants.

WHITE GRUBS are the large, thick-bodied larvae of May beetles, also called June beetles in northern states. Larvae feed on the roots of plants, including strawberries. Avoid planting strawberries in newly turned sod.

DISEASES
∾

Diseases can cause as much damage as insects do. In fact, severe diseases can defoliate plants and cause most of the fruit to drop. Here's a list of the most common diseases so that you can spot them early and apply the necessary fungicide to control the problem.

ANTHRACNOSE is a fungus disease of raspberries. It affects mostly the purple and black varieties. It is characterized on canes and leaves by round or oval spots with a brown, red, or purple border and gray center. Spots are up to half an inch in diameter. Clean cultivation, which promotes air circulation, helps control this disease.

LEAF SPOT is a common disease in currants. Infected leaves develop numerous small, round spots with gray centers. This disease frequently causes leaves to fall early. Rake and, if possible, burn the leaves.

POWDERY MILDEW infects many plants and is occasionally serious on currants. It causes a white moldy growth that distorts leaves and stem tips.

SPUR BLIGHT in raspberries is a fungus disease characterized by purplish oval spots around the buds. Infected areas are weakened, and fruit production is reduced.

PEST-CONTROL GUIDELINES

When to spray or dust is just as important as what to apply in order to control harmful insects and plant diseases. Some areas have more insect problems than others and different types of pests. Seasons are different too. One year you may have lots of rain, which requires more attention to cover sprays to prevent mildews, spots, and rusts on trees and fruit bushes or vines. And if you get heavy rains after spraying, you may need to spray again to reapply the material washed off.

Every county extension agent in every county in every state all across America has a suggested, tested, approved spray schedule. Your best bet is to check with your local agent for the recommended materials, application rates, and timing that have proved most effective in your area.

When you grow fruit and berries, you may find that they bear more abundantly than you anticipated. For exam-

ple, a 50-foot row of black-berries can yield more than 100 quarts of berries. Blue-berries, too, have a habit of bearing abundantly after they have established a strong roothold.

If you're lucky, your big-gest problem may be that you have more fruit than you can eat or give away. The answer to your prob-lem may be to make your own homemade jams, jel-lies, and preserves.

JAMS, JELLIES,

AND

PRESERVES

Homemade preserves, jam, and jelly are easy to make. The ingredients are simply sugar and fruit. Your method of preparing the fruit and the way it is processed determine what the finished product will be. For example, if you use sugar and whole berries, you get preserves or jam. If you strain the fruit juices and sweet-en them, you get jelly. Actually, there is a bit more to the process, but the methods are easy to follow and the results are delicious.

The size of the fresh fruit, its state of ripeness, and its variety all determine the amount of preserved fruit you will get, but the following chart gives you a general idea of how much to expect when you preserve the fruits of your gardening fun.

FRUIT	AMOUNT	YIELD
Berries*	1 crate (24 quarts)	32–36 pints
	1 1/2 pints	1 pint
Currants	2 quarts	4 pints
	3/4 pound	1 pint
Raspberries	1 crate (24 pints)	24 pints
	1 pint	1 pint
Strawberries	1 crate (24 quarts)	38 pints
	2/3 quart	1 pint

*Includes blackberries, blueberries, dewberries, elderberries, and gooseberries.

The most important rule in making preserves, jams, and jellies is to make small amounts. That way the critical timings for boiling and mixing can be followed properly and the results will be much more successful. If any burning occurs, a burned flavor can permeate that entire batch. Also, fruits tend to crush and stick to cooking vessels if large batches are made, which can reduce the quality of the finished product.

This chapter provides general directions for each category of fruit preserving. These can be varied with recipes from your favorite cookbooks and from friends and neighbors.

PRESERVING TIPS
ᴄᴡ

Preserves are made by cooking small whole fruits or uniformly sized pieces of larger fruits in a syrup until the fruit is saturated. When the preserves are done, the fruit should be almost its original size and the syrup should be medium to thick.

Always select ripe, firm fruit. Discard any that are bruised or have signs of mold or other blemishes. You may leave berries whole and slice or cut larger fruits into bite-sized pieces.

The next step is to weigh the prepared fruit and the sugar, exactly as prescribed in the recipe. After the first batch, you can adjust the recipe for more sweetness or less, according to your own personal taste. Proportions range slightly above or below ¾ pound of sugar to 1 pound of fruit, based on your own sweet tooth.

Prepare the syrup by bringing the sugar and fruit juice—or sugar and water, if you are using larger fruit pieces—to a rolling boil. Then add the prepared fruit that you have preweighed. Cook rapidly in an open kettle until the fruit is clear and translucent. At this point, the syrup should be just under the jell stage. This stage is reached at about 222°F, which you can observe by using a jam and jelly thermometer. If you prefer not to use a thermometer, try this: Cool a spoonful of syrup in a saucer and test the consistency. It should be reasonably thick and not too runny. Overcooked syrup is somewhat gummy. After a test or two, you will quickly learn how to spot the right consistency.

When cooking is done, remove the fruit carefully from the syrup and place the fruit in a dish or enamel pan. Don't let the foam that may form stick to the fruit. It won't harm the final product, but it is unattractive. After the fruit is removed, skim off any remaining foam in the syrup and then pour the syrup over the fruit. Cover with a cloth to let it cool thoroughly. During cooling, the fruit will absorb much of the syrup.

While the fruit is cooling, sterilize your glass jars by boiling them for 10 to 15 minutes. Prepare the tops according to the manufacturer's directions. Ball, Kerr, or other standard canning jars and their special closure lids are recommended. They ensure tight, permanent seals that reduce spoilage problems.

When your jars are sterilized, return the cooled fruit and syrup to a clean kettle and bring the mixture back to the boiling point. Do not recook the mixture or you will get some sticking and possibly burning. Ladle the hot fruit into the sterilized jars. Remember to keep the jars warm, or you risk their cracking when you pour the hot fruit and syrup into cold jars. Next, add syrup to fill the jar to within half an inch of the top. That space is necessary for the final stage of processing. Remove any air bubbles at this time by sliding a clean kitchen knife inside the jar and around the edges. If you don't, bubbles will rise and the syrup will settle so that it may not cover the fruit properly. This could cause the top layer to turn dark and become unappealing in appearance. Next, wipe the top of the jar and adjust the lid. Then place the jars of preserves into hot water and process at the simmering point, 180°F, for 10 minutes.

After the 10 minutes of simmering, remove the jars carefully. Put them on wire racks or place them slightly apart on a cutting board and let them cool naturally. Never put hot jars on a cool surface, because the bottoms might crack. Keep the jars slightly apart so that air circulates freely. Don't try to cool them quickly—not even tempered glass jars—by pouring water on them; this could loosen the seal or even cause jars to burst.

If you are using lids that require extra tightening after processing, do that as soon as you remove them from the simmering water, or as the manufacturer's directions suggest. Use a warm, damp cloth for a better grip and to avoid burned fingers.

When the jars are cool, store them in a cool, dark, dry area. Warmth and light can reduce the quality; moisture can rust metal lids.

These are basic guidelines. Always follow the manufacturer's instructions for proper use of particular types of jars. Below are some old standard recipes you might like to try as you tune up your preserve-making talents.

GRAPE PRESERVES

■ Take 5 pounds of grapes and separate the hulls and pulp. Heat the pulp to the boiling point. Then put the pulp through a sieve to remove seeds. Add deseeded grape pulp to grape hulls and cook slowly until the hulls are tender—about 15 minutes. Add water if necessary. Then add 5 pounds of sugar directly to the simmering hulls and pulp. Cook until the mixture reaches the light jell stage. Then follow general directions for making preserves.

STRAWBERRY PRESERVES

■ Use 2 pounds of berries, 2 pounds of sugar, and 1½ cups of berry juice or water. Wash, cap, and stem the strawberries. Make a syrup of the sugar and juice or water, and add the berries. Cook until the berries are clear and the syrup is thick. Pack into jars and process. If the berries become translucent before the syrup is thick enough, simply remove the fruit to a bowl or pan and continue cooking the syrup until it thickens sufficiently.

JAM-MAKING TIPS
ℭ

Jams are often confused with preserves. Preserves use as much whole fruit as possible, but jams use crushed or cooked fruit so that the final product assumes a consistency closer to jelly. In other words, jam is about halfway between preserves and jelly. It should be semifirm but not runny, and pieces of fruit should be obvious in it.

You can use the same fruits for both jams and preserves, but bear this in mind: Riper, less firm fruits are better for jam making. Size, shape, and texture don't hold up as well if you attempt to make preserves from fully ripe fruit. Jam is the answer when your crop comes in abundantly and you want to use several methods to spread that tasty harvest over the months ahead.

As a general rule, for each pound of fruit, use ¾ pound of sugar. Place the fruit and sugar in a pot or kettle and add enough water or fruit juice to avoid burning.

As you cook, stir and mash the fruit to release juices and let the sugar penetrate the fruit well. Cook slowly until the mixture forms a thick mass, at about 222°F. When the jam reaches the desired consistency, ladle or pour it into hot sterilized jars to within half an inch of the top. Remove any air bubbles on the sides with a clean kitchen knife. Then adjust the lid properly. Place the jars of jam into hot water and process for 10 minutes at the simmering point of 180°F. Remove the jars and tighten the lids, if necessary.

After the jars are thoroughly cool (several hours or overnight), store them in a dark, cool, dry closet or cool room. Be sure to label the jars with variety, date, sugar amount, and any other information you want to note.

BLACKBERRY JAM

■ Select firm, juicy berries and wash them well. Use 1 pound of fruit to ¾ pound of sugar. Follow directions for jam making.

GRAPE JAM

■ Wash grapes and remove the stems. Separate hulls from pulp. Cook the pulp until seeds can be removed by pressing fruit through a colander. Boil the hulls with a little water until they are tender, and then add the pulp. For each pound of fruit use ¾ pound of sugar. Follow directions for jam making.

STRAWBERRY AND RASPBERRY JAM

■ Wash and cap berries. For each pound of fruit, use ¾ pound of sugar. Follow directions of jam making.

Jelly is sweetened fruit juice that is cooked until the jell stage is reached. It should be clear, free from slices and bits of fruit, yet firm enough so that its shape is retained when you cut it or scoop it out. Making jelly takes a bit of practice to perfect your skills in order to produce a consistently clear, firm texture. But after a few small batches you should have the process down pat.

For jelly, use only firm, ripe fruits. Underripe or overripe fruits do not contain the proper amounts of acid and pectin needed for jelly. Some varieties have more pectin than others, so you may need to add one of the commercially available jelling products if the natural fruit pectin isn't sufficient.

Cook the fruit in as little water as possible to extract the juice. Each type of fruit requires somewhat different cooking times. Watch the time carefully, since overcooking destroys the natural pectin. Next, strain the juice from the fruit by placing the fruit in cheesecloth over a bowl or pot. Secure the cheesecloth with large rubber bands. For the clearest jelly, let the juice seep through without pressing. Then put the juice into a jelly bag for re-straining. These bags are available at hardware stores and other suppliers, including the major mail-order firms.

At this stage, test the fruit juice at room temperature using a jelmeter. A jelmeter is a graduated glass tube with an opening at each end. The rate of flow of juice through this tube measures its jelling power. It tells you whether additional pectin is needed and gives you an index for the amount of sugar to be added during cooking. Always use granulated sugar because brown sugar or other types of sweeteners may discolor the jelly and overpower the fruit's natural flavor.

Measure the juice and sugar next and combine them in a large enough kettle or pot to permit rapid boiling. Because precise timing is needed for jelly, it is best to do small quantities, about 3 to 4 cups of juice at a time. Bring the mixture to a rapid boil. A jelly thermometer is helpful. The juice and sugar should reach the jell stage at about 222°F. You can also try the spoon test: Dip out a spoonful of the liquid and tip the spoon. If the jelly still drips, it needs a bit more boiling. If it holds together in one or two large, bloblike drips, it is ready.

As soon as this stage is reached, remove the jelly from the heat and skim off any foam. Pour the jelly immediately into presterilized hot jelly jars. Have melted paraffin ready, and pour a thin coat of melted wax on top of the jelly and secure the lid. Allow the jars to cool slowly, then store them in a dark, cool, dry place.

You can also make jelly stock and store it until you have more time for the complete jelly-making process. When large quantities of fruit are ripening at one time, just making the stock lets you put more stock aside quickly.

Following are recipes for blackberry and grape jelly stock and the jelly itself.

BLACKBERRY JELLY

■ Wash 6 quarts of blackberries and crush them well. Add about 1 pint of water, if needed. Boil for 15 minutes and strain through double cheesecloth.

To make blackberry jelly, use 3 to 4 cups of strained stock. Test the juice to determine the amount of sugar to use. Combine sugar and juice and boil rapidly. Follow the general jelly-making directions.

GRAPE JELLY

■ Crush 8 pounds of grapes. Add 1 pint or up to 1 quart water, if needed. Boil for 20 minutes. Strain through cheesecloth and pour the juice through a flannel bag.

To make grape jelly, strain the juice carefully to remove cream of tartar crystals. Test the juice to determine the amount of sugar to use. Combine sugar and juice and boil rapidly. Follow the general jelly-making directions.

From these basic steps, you can expand your skills with a variety of other recipes and combinations. In fact, you can even branch out into marmalades, conserves, and fruit butters if you like. Cookbooks provide a wealth of recipes for the adventurous fruit grower.

YIELD CHART

It's nice to know before you plant how much your bush friuts will yield. Here's a handy chart that I've found to be quite accurate.

	MINIMUM DISTANCE BETWEEN ROWS/PLANTS (FEET)	AVERAGE ANNUAL YIELD PER PLANT (QUARTS)	BEARING LIFE (YEARS)	AGE EXPECTANCY (YEARS)
Blueberry	6/4	4	3	20–30
Blackberry (erect)	8/3	1 $^1/_2$	1	5–12
Blackberry (trailing)	8/6	1 $^1/_2$	1	5–12
Raspberry (red)	8/3	1 $^1/_2$	1	5–12
Raspberry (black)	8/4	1 $^1/_2$	1	5–12
Raspberry (purple)	8/3	1 $^1/_2$	1	5–12
Grape (American) (French American)	10/8	12	3	20–30
Grape (muscadine)	10/10	18	3	20–30
Strawberry (regular)	3/1	$^1/_2$	1	3
Strawberry (everbearing)	3/1	$^1/_2$	$^1/_3$	3
Currant	8/4	5	3	10–20
Gooseberry	8/4	5	3	10–20

SUPPLIERS OF FRUIT TREES, SHRUBS, AND PLANTS

Here's a list of leading nurseries and mail-order firms that have been supplying fruit trees, shrubs, and plants to American gardeners for many years. Their reputations are well established. Many of these firms have beautifully illustrated catalogs for free or at a nominal cost.

Bountiful Ridge Nurseries
Princess Anne, Maryland 21853

W. Atlee Burpee Co.
300 Park Avenue
Warminster, Pennsylvania 18974

Burgess Seed & Plant Company
Galesburg, Michigan 49053

Cumberland Valley Nurseries, Inc.
McMinnville, Tennessee 37110

Emlong Nurseries, Inc.
Stevensville, Michigan 49127

Farmer Seed & Nursery Co.
Faribault, Minnesota 55021

Earl Ferris Nursery
Hampton, Iowa 50441

Henry Field Seed & Nursery Co.
Shenandoah, Iowa 51601

Gurney Seed & Nursery Co.
Yankton, South Dakota 57078

Hillemeyer Nurseries
Lexington, Kentucky 40500

Inter-State Nurseries, Inc.
Hamburg, Iowa 51640

Kelly Bros. Nurseries
Dansville, New York 14437

J. E. Miller Nurseries
Canandaigua, New York 14424

Monroe Nursery Company
Monroe, Michigan 48161

New York State Fruit Testing Cooperative Association
Geneva, New York 14456

Ozark Nursery
Tahlequah, Oklahoma 74464

R. H. Shumway
Rockford, Illinois 61100

Stark Bros. Nurseries
Louisiana, Missouri 63353

There are many others, some small and selling locally or selling only those varieties that perform best in their own areas. In general, the firms that have been growing and selling fruit and berry bushes nationally for many years can provide a wider choice of varieties to suit your needs. Local garden centers, nurseries, and farm supply stores also have stock available in season.

SOURCES

Your best bet for additional information about fruit growing in specific areas is the agricultural extension office in states with major fruit-producing regions (listed below). Address your inquiries to the agricultural extension service director. If you live out-of-state, you can expect to pay a slight charge for mailing.

New York State College of
Agriculture and Life Sciences
Ithaca, New York 14850

Rutgers University
The State University of New Jersey
New Brunswick, New Jersey 08903

Michigan State University
East Lansing, Michigan 48823

University of Illinois
Urbana, Illinois 61801

University of Massachusetts
Amherst, Massachusetts 02002

Ohio State University
Columbus, Ohio 43210

New York State Agricultural
Experiment Station
Geneva, New York 14456

Of course you can also check sources in your own state. The Cooperative Extension Service of each state is a federal- and state-funded organization that can be a highly valuable resource. State extension specialists are charged with the responsibility of providing information to homeowners and citizens in their states. In addition, each county in the United States has county extension specialists. These people are well trained in providing detailed information about fruit trees, berry bushes and plants, home ground planting, and horticulture in general. Every state also has a land-grant agricultural college as part of its state university system. At these colleges you can consult a variety of horticultural specialists. Listed below are the addresses of the land-grant colleges and universities. From that source you can get the names and addresses of county specialists. Address your inquiries to the Agricultural Information Office at the following:

Auburn University
Auburn, Alabama 36830

University of Alaska
College, Alaska 99701

College of Agriculture
University of Arizona
Tucson, Arizona 85721

University of Arkansas
Box 391
Little Rock, Arkansas 72203

Agricultural Extension Service
2200 University Avenue
Berkeley, California 94720

Colorado State University
Fort Collins, Colorado 80521

College of Agriculture
University of Connecticut
Storrs, Connecticut 06268

College of Agricultural Sciences
University of Delaware
Newark, Delaware 19711

University of Florida
217 Rolfs Hall
Gainesville, Florida 32601

College of Agriculture
University of Georgia
Athens, Georgia 30602

University of Hawaii
2500 Dole Street
Honolulu, Hawaii 96822

College of Agriculture
University of Idaho
Moscow, Idaho 83843

College of Agriculture
University of Illinois
Urbana, Illinois 61801

Agricultural Administration Building
Purdue University
Lafayette, Indiana 47907

Iowa State University
Ames, Iowa 50010

Kansas State University
Manhattan, Kansas 66502

College of Agriculture
University of Kentucky
Lexington, Kentucky 40506

Louisiana State University
Knapp Hall
University Station
Baton Rouge, Louisiana 70803

University of Maine
Orono, Maine 04473

University of Maryland
Agricultural Division
College Park, Maryland 20742

Stockbridge Hall
University of Massachusetts
Amherst, Massachusetts 01002
Michigan State University
109 Agricultural Hall
East Lansing, Michigan 48823

Institute of Agriculture
University of Minnesota
St. Paul, Minnesota 55101

Mississippi State University
State College, Mississippi 39762

University of Missouri
1-98 Agricultural Building
Columbia, Missouri 65201

Montana State University
Bozeman, Montana 59715

College of Agriculture
University of Nebraska
Lincoln, Nebraska 68503

University of Nevada
Reno, Nevada 89507

University of New Hampshire
Schofield Hall
Durham, New Hampshire 03824

College of Agriculture
Rutgers—The State University
New Brunswick, New Jersey 08903

New Mexico State University
Drawer 3A1
Las Cruces, New Mexico 88001
State College of Agriculture
Cornell University
Ithaca, New York 14850

North Carolina State University
State College Station
Raleigh, North Carolina 27607

North Dakota State University
State University Station
Fargo, North Dakota 58102

Ohio State University
2120 Fyffe Road
Columbus, Ohio 43210

Oklahoma State University
Stillwater, Oklahoma 74074

Oregon State University
Carvallis, Oregon 97331

Pennsylvania State University
Room 1, Armsby Building
University Park, Pennsylvania 16802

University of Puerto Rico
Mayaguez Campus, Box AR
Rio Piedras, Puerto Rico 00928

University of Rhode Island
16 Woodwall Hall
Kingston, Rhode Island 02881

Clemson University
Clemson, South Carolina 29631
South Dakota State University
University Station
Brookings, South Dakota 57006

University of Tennessee
Box 1071
Knoxville, Tennessee 37901

Texas A & M University
College Station, Texas 77843

Utah State University
Logan, Utah 84321

University of Vermont
Burlington, VT 05401

Virginia Polytechnic Institute
Blacksburg, Virginia 24061

Washington State University
115 Wilson Hall
Pullman, Washington 99163

West Virginia University
Evansdale Campus
Appalachian Center
Morgantown, West Virginia 26506

University of Wisconsin
Madison, Wisconsin 53706

University of Wyoming
Box 3354
Laramie, Wyoming 82070

Federal Extension Service
U. S. Department of Agriculture
Washington, D.C. 20250

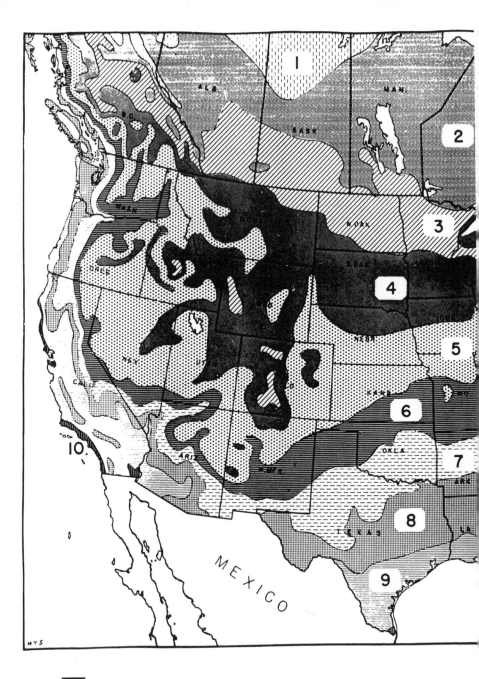

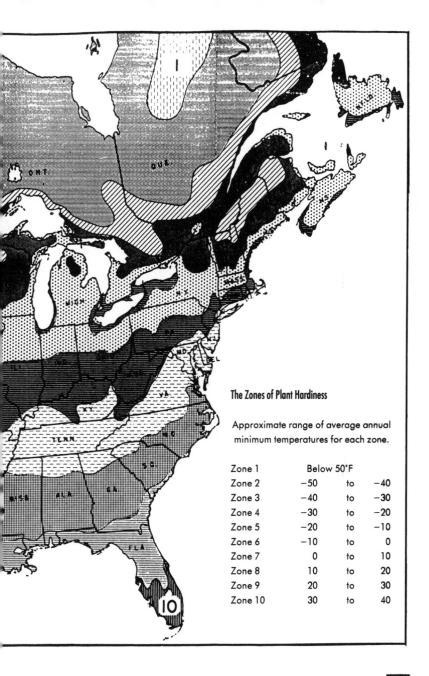

The Zones of Plant Hardiness

Approximate range of average annual minimum temperatures for each zone.

Zone 1	Below 50°F		
Zone 2	−50	to	−40
Zone 3	−40	to	−30
Zone 4	−30	to	−20
Zone 5	−20	to	−10
Zone 6	−10	to	0
Zone 7	0	to	10
Zone 8	10	to	20
Zone 9	20	to	30
Zone 10	30	to	40

U.S. Agricultural Research Service, 30

U.S. Department of Agriculture, 7, 24, 94
  Research Station (Beltsville, Maryland), 78

umbrella system (grape-growing), 72

water table, 42

weeds, 26, 85, 103
  as compost material, 11; as robbers of soil nutrients, 42

white grubs (larvae of May or June beetles), 109

winterkill, 85

youngberries. *See* dewberries